Remodeling
Old Houses

REMODELING OLD HOUSES

Without Destroying Their Character

by GEORGE STEPHEN

Illustrated by the Author

1972

ALFRED A. KNOPF

New York

THIS IS A BORZOI BOOK
PUBLISHED BY ALFRED A. KNOPF, INC.

ISBN: hardcover 0–394–47537–2
         paperback 0–394–70756–7

Library of Congress Catalog Card Number: 74–171124

Manufactured in the United States of America

First Edition

To Veronika

ACKNOWLEDGMENTS

Many of the ideas in this book grew out of material originally prepared for a series of talks that were part of the three courses for rehabilitation specialists held at the Massachusetts Bay Community College from 1968 until 1970 and sponsored by a Demonstration Grant from the U.S. Department of Housing and Urban Development. I would like to thank the students in these courses, who, by the genuine interest they showed in rehabilitation design, persuaded me that it was a "teachable" subject, and to acknowledge a special debt of gratitude to the director, Professor George C. Rogers, Jr., of the M.B.C.C. faculty, who was the first to suggest the possibility of this book and to prod me into doing something about it.

I would also like to thank Mr. Robert Grant Neiley, architect, of Boston and Mr. Richard A. Lockhart, urban planner, of Cambridge for their comments and suggestions for improving the text, Mr. Robert B. Rettig, project director of the Boston Landmarks Commission, for his help with some of the trickier definitions and problems related to historical accuracy, many of my colleagues of the Boston Redevelopment Authority, who from time to time came up with useful pieces of information that have found their way into the book, and Mrs. Yvonne Ronchinsky for her generous help in preparing the first manuscript.

Finally, my thanks to Dr. Walter Muir Whitehill, director of the Boston Athenaeum, for his encouragement of the project and good advice regarding the publishing of the book, and to Mrs. Jane Garrett of Alfred A. Knopf, Inc., at whose suggestion some important chapters were added and the book increased in usefulness.

Contents

ix

🕸️|*Introduction*

This book is intended as a guide for all those concerned with the rehabilitation or remodeling of old—though not necessarily "historical"—houses or apartments. The language has been kept as free as possible from obscure technical terms so that it can be read, hopefully with pleasure, by nonprofessionals as well as professionals. Such technical terms as are used will be found in the brief glossary.

Much has been written about the financial and legal side of rehabilitation and also about the techniques of historic restoration, but little has been said about the other everyday architectural problems that face those who want to alter a house, say less than one hundred years old, so that it better serves the needs of modern living but retains the best parts of its original character.

This book, therefore, will be mainly about how good rehabilitation should *look* and how it should *work*.

Sadly enough, in the design of smaller rehabilitation jobs (as well as in the design of new houses) the professional designer—the architect—is all too often not involved. The reason for this is simple: it is legally possible in such situations to build without an architect, but not without a builder—at least for the plumbing and electrical work—so when the budget is tight, the first "saving" is the architect's fee. This often turns out to be false economy, however, since many of the wrong things that can be done to an old building also happen to be expensive, and simply by avoiding these mistakes a good architect can save his client's money for better things. Also, when working on an hourly basis, as is common on rehabilitation jobs, the architect has nothing to gain personally by increasing the cost of the construction work. Most important is the fact that the chances of ending up with something attractive and efficient are greatly increased by employing someone specifically trained to design.

Assuming, however, that much rehabilitation will continue to be done "without benefit of architect," this book is addressed mainly to the home owner and to the building contractor—those who are in effect doing the designing—as well as to all others interested in giving new life to old buildings. (Perhaps even some architects may steal a look, or hide a copy under their drawing boards.)

The book has been divided, as far as possible, into self-contained sections so that those seeking specific information can get it easily. It is hoped, however, that those who are simply interested in older houses in general, and how they can be remodeled with kindness, will find interesting and useful information throughout, concerning all aspects of the design and building processes connected with rehabilitation —even, for the benefit of would-be architects, the way to execute some of the drawing. Furthermore, such information as how to identify some of the rather puzzling nineteenth-century architectural revival styles has been included in an effort to make this not just a "how-to," but also a "why-to" book.

Because this book attempts to address a wide range of people with varied backgrounds and specific interests, it is unavoidable that a few intelligences will be insulted from time to time, and the author humbly asks in advance the reader's understanding and forgiveness if this should happen.

To date, the rehabilitation of old or "middle-aged" houses and buildings has not always been associated with good standards of architectural design. In many cases, of course, the fact that some attempt has been to save an older house is in itself commendable and it may seem ungenerous to apply architectural yardsticks to the result. The author believes, however, that good design can be achieved in most instances by the average person on a limited budget if he is interested in going about things in the right way. Therefore, in addition to discussing the good points and positive advantages of an old house, this book will lay considerable emphasis on just what is meant by "good design" and—most important—how its principles apply to each of the details in typical rehabilitation situations.

The book, in short, is for those who want to give new life to old houses and care enough about them to want to do it well.

Remodeling Old Houses

I
Why Rehabilitate?
Why Design?

The Background

Throughout history it has been the lot of each generation to live in an environment that has been largely designed or determined for it by its predecessors. The present is no exception, and many of us, whether we are aware of it or not, either live or work in surroundings dominated by buildings at least over fifty years old—and most of these put up by our Victorian grandfathers or great-grandfathers about a hundred years ago.

This predominance of nineteenth-century architecture is no accident, for it was a time of extensive and optimistic building. In many countries, including America, which early led the field in the industrial revolution, towns became cities and cities became metropolises in a comparatively short time in the latter part of the century, not only by the building-up of the older urban cores but also by the addition of vast suburbs to provide the extra housing necessary for the population explosions in the new centers of work. In sheer quantity of houses built, nothing like it had ever happened before. Workers streamed in from the countryside and from Europe to the new urban job centers, and at the same time the growing middle classes pushed outward to the new suburbs now made accessible to the city by first horse-drawn streetcars, and later the electrically powered ones.

Houses in the new suburbs were built in a range of styles, according to the income and status of the intended owners. The row house, which up until this time had been associated with gracious urban living, declined in popularity and was seldom seen. (Some good examples continued to be built in the cities, however, and are now much sought after with the recent rediscovery of the "town house" as a desirable way of life.) The suburban styles often began with the double or triple dwelling-unit house standing close with its similar or identical neighbors on a narrow lot, the general effect approaching to row houses from the outside. Internally the layout was different, since light could be introduced to more rooms because of the extra windows on the side wall. This type, together with the narrow-lot single house, was found in the inner suburbs and built for the less affluent—the cost of commuting being an important factor.

After this there was a whole range of subtle gradations as the commuting radius increased, the size of the lots and the houses becoming larger and the architectural treatment richer, until the great mansions of the wealthy in the outer suburbs were reached. Many of these are now surrounded by houses of less exalted status that were built after the original estates had been divided into smaller lots later in the nineteenth century.

As a result of this activity we have become heirs to a huge legacy of residential architecture of all shapes and sizes—which is suffering to various degrees from the neglect commonly shown to things that are neither very old nor new—and which, for better or for worse, determines the quality of much of our environment. We are only beginning to understand that this legacy contains untold wealth in the form of generous spaces and graceful details—much of it now almost impossible to reproduce at any price—and it lies waiting to be claimed by those who are aware of it.

The interest that at last is being shown the environment, regarding such subjects as ecology, conservation, and urban planning, must also include an active and intelligent interest in our architectural legacy if it is to make any sense.

Why Rehabilitate?

Until quite recently, nineteenth-century or Victorian buildings were on the far side of an unusually wide "generation gap" and regarded by architects and public alike as old-fashioned, unfunctional, or just in quaintly bad taste. With the coming of age of twentieth-century architecture, however, the attitude toward the immediate past has become more relaxed and charitable, and the nineteenth-century house is becoming valued for the qualities just mentioned—spaciousness and interest of detail—plus its durability, excellent construction, and just plain livability —qualities that are hard to come by in our own cost-conscious times.

The following illustration is an extreme but accurate comparison of the relative values of the nineteenth and twentieth centuries, as represented by typical structures from each era set side-by-side in an urban environment.

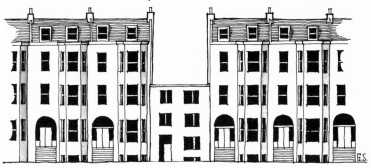

The older houses are four and a half Victorian floors (or forty-five to fifty feet) above the sidewalk, with generous entrance stairs and an imposing verticality in general proportions. By contrast the new house, which tries to fill the gap in the middle, can rise, by modern standards, only three mid-twentieth-century floors (or twenty-five to twenty-seven feet) without having an expensive elevator installed; therefore it cannot relate externally in any way to its neighbors and it seems to express its discomfiture by the unsatisfying proportions.

It can be argued that the new building above is not representative of the best in current architecture, which is certainly true. However, the point is that it is representative of the average; since "average" new buildings vastly outnumber "good" new buildings, no further argument should be necessary to convince ourselves of the desirability of saving as much of the better nineteenth-century work as possible and adapting it to current needs.

The word "adapting" is the key. We are all familiar with the view of the past that relegates it to the museum and have visited and admired those restored Colonial or Federal style mansions where one wipes the dust of the twentieth century from one's feet before entering. In cities such places are often further segregated from everyday life by the removal of their original surroundings—such as Carpenter's Hall in Philadelphia, which floats in a green vacuum. It is not enough, however, to embalm a few lucky survivors from a more distant past as token "history" and to ignore the potentials of thousands of more recent structures to be active—and attractive—members of the living community by sympathetic rehabilitation.

Old buildings—like old people—are essential to a healthy and mature society in that they give a sense of balance and continuity with the past, but *they must be valued at their true worth and not merely accepted on sufferance.*

Last, but not least, it must be stressed that as well as being desirable from an architectural and historical point of view *good rehabilitation work can make good economic sense.* Even the most expensive type of rehabilitation work rarely equals the cost of new work of a comparable standard, and in the more moderately priced work, the bonuses already mentioned in the form of generous spaces and elegant details can give a return far in excess of the money involved. Those who may still be inclined to doubt this should look again at the minimum gap house in the last illustration, which would almost certainly cost much more to build than it would to rehabilitate one of the neighboring houses—even without adding the possible cost of demolishing the old structure to make room for the new one.

Some Techniques and Definitions

At this point it might be useful to describe briefly some of the ways in which older buildings can be reinstated or retained as active members of the architectural community and to mention some of the things—both good and bad—that happen to them. This will also help clear the air by defining some of the basic terms used.

Preservation is one of the words most frequently used in connection with old buildings—so much so that it is often used loosely to describe the entire range of the nicer things that can happen to them. In a way this is true, in that everything from strict restoration to fairly extensive redesign is a way of "preserving." In the technical sense, however, preservation means keeping the building in its existing form while at the same time taking measures to prevent further deterioration of the structure. A different or more appropriate use may be found for the building, but the appearance will remain essentially the same. This is a useful technique for rescuing buildings of historic interest without necessarily making them into museums. In the case of nineteenth-century houses, however, it is likely to concern us less than other alternatives.

The techniques that will be of most direct concern can be conveniently summed up in three "Rs"—*Restoration, Rehabilitation,* and *Redesign.* These concepts cover everything from the returning of the building to its original form to its being almost completely rebuilt with little or nothing of the original structure or style visible. These, of course, are extremes and in between is a whole range of valid possibilities covered by the term *Rehabilitation.* The terms *Remodeling* and *Renovation* can be included within *Rehabilitation* for all practical purposes and will be dealt with under that heading.

Restoration—or returning a building, as much as possible, to its original appearance and condition—is a technique used mainly on buildings of outstanding historical or architectural interest. It can be very expensive, often involving the removal of details and additions made at later dates and the reproduction of details for replacement which are no longer available "off the shelf" as it were (if indeed they ever were!). In buildings over one hundred years old missing items such as a cornice may have to be reconstructed from clues like contemporary engravings, verbal descriptions, or fragments of the original found perhaps in the building itself—research which can lend exciting overtones of sleuth work to otherwise painstaking labor.

Needless to say, if the building is to be lived in, total restoration is impossible, since few of us would care to rely on eighteenth-century plumbing, open fireplaces, and candles for our utilities. In other words, *total restoration is only possible when the building is to be a museum piece.* This fact should be pondered well by all so-called purists who raise their hands in horror at the sight of an undisguisedly modern interior within a restored exterior—a combination that has been effectively used by the best architects in our own time and throughout history.

Restoration, then, is almost always a compromise and ranges from almost total restoration where only the essential services are modernized to restoration of only a part of the building when the exterior, perhaps, or a particular part of the interior, is of historic or architectural interest. When sensitively handled, such combinations of old and new architectural styles can be very attractive and exciting—effectively setting each other off, just as carefully selected old and new furniture sharing the same room can do.

While on the subject of restoration a few words must be said about "pre-dating," or making a building look as though it belongs to a period older than its actual age. This is often done to certain Victorian houses by installing Colonial-type doors and small-paned "six-over-six" windows. If the detailing and proportions are good, the result can be a harmless white lie, but if they are not—which is more often the case—a simple and charming house can be made overnight to look like a catalogue of parts available at the local lumber yard. This type of "historical" veneer is widely used by the marginal speculator-builder to cover up shoddy materials and disguise bad proportions and should have no place in honest work, whether in new building or rehabilitation. Good work, too, is often marred by the application of such "instant history," and many landlords rely on its snob appeal to rent apartments in marginal districts.

Those who have any genuine love for the past should learn to distinguish between the real and the fake: it's not how old the house is, but how well it looks that matters— or to put it in other terms, there's no point in boasting of one's ancestry if the family is going to the dogs!

Rehabilitation—the second "R" and hereafter often referred to simply as rehab—means literally "making habitable or useful again." Although a rather cumbersome word, it describes conveniently a wide range of approaches toward the improvement of the nineteenth-century house from simply a new paint job to extensive external or internal reconstruction. It is often confused with restoration, but whereas the latter can be considered the "historical" or antiquarian approach, rehabilitation may entail the introduction of new elements that are nonhistorical but that, if well designed in themselves, can relate well to the older parts of the building. Rehab may include some restoration or, on the other hand, may change the building entirely. Being such a comprehensive term it will be used often in this book.

In the interest of variety, the terms *Remodeling* and *Renovation*, which cover much of the ground of rehabilitation, will be sometimes used in this book in place of "rehabilitation."

Redesign—the third "R"—is at the opposite end of the scale from restoration. Here the original structure often is so altered as to be indistinguishable from a new building. This approach can be appropriate if the existing building is of inferior design, built of inferior materials, or if intended to be used for a purpose totally different from that for which it was originally designed, such as in the conversion of an industrial building to an apartment house.

The following diagram attempts to illustrate the complete spectrum of possibilities for improving older houses, showing how the three "Rs" relate to each other.

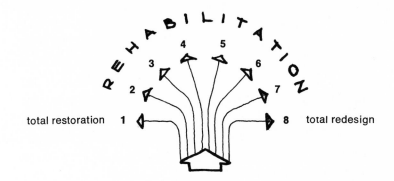

Translating some of these alternatives into job descriptions and reading clockwise, the list might be as follows:

Total Restoration	1. The house as a museum piece in itself and not lived in
Restoration	2. Almost-complete restoration with new plumbing and services
Partial Restoration	3. Restoration of outside only, with completely modern interior
Rehabilitation	4. Some restoration plus a paint job
	5. Repairs, cleaning, and painting
	6. Same with some alterations
	7. Same with more extensive alterations or additions
Redesign	8. End result looks like a new building

The exact order of these descriptions will, of course, vary —particularly in the middle of the range, where in some cases "repairs, cleaning, and painting" may result in almost total restoration—but the important thing to remember is that *all of these approaches are valid if they are done well.*

Some mention must be made of the less pleasant things that can happen to an old house (aside from bad "improvement" that is—a fate which may be worse than death!), and the most common of these are neglect and demolition.

Neglect can often be remedied by action, but demolition is a value judgment often open to question. The usual reasons for proposing demolition are:

1. Neglect has gone beyond the economic point of no return.
2. The owner wants something new in place of something "old-fashioned."
3. A complete change of use is proposed by the owner for the land, the site perhaps being more valuable than the building.
4. The building cannot be assimilated in the official urban plan for the neighborhood.

There is not enough space to go into all the factors that have a bearing on what can be a most difficult decision, but an owner contemplating demolition should be urged to take a long hard look at what he has—particularly if he just wants "something new"—lest what he may charitably intend as a sort of "mercy killing" becomes another architectural murder. Often the least likely candidates for rehabilitation turn out to be the most interesting and successful when completed, and in the end the owner has something of unique worth with which to confound the skeptics.

In connection with urban plans, it should be mentioned that planners have become more rehabilitation-conscious of late and, with hope, the era of the wholesale use of the wrecker's ball is over. Many cities, disillusioned with the physical and social results of the era of "slum clearance," now call for extensive rehabilitation of the best of what exists rather than relying on total new development programs, which all-too-often result in an overdose of high-rise structures of an architectural quality somewhat lower than either the buildings or the rents.

Before leaving our definitions there is one term that must receive passing mention—*Modernization.* The word is a perfectly legitimate one, which can be used to describe certain improvements that can reasonably be made in old buildings, but through unfortunate associations it has become anathema to many people who have a genuine regard for architectural quality. It has been too often identified with such details as the so-called picture window so cheerfully and incongruously punched through the wall of a nineteenth-century house, or with the extensive use of "natural-finish" aluminum for windows, doors, and trim, and other such unfortunate design choices, which will be discussed in later chapters. Be understanding, therefore, of a sudden haggard look in the eye of the architect to whom you may be talking, and be sparing in the use of the term—at least in his presence!

Why Design?

Although architects may be the only designers in the sense that they are *consciously* shaping the end result, in point of fact any decision that affects the usefulness or the appearance of a building—no matter who makes it—is a design decision. It may take the form of a layout idea sketched on the back of an envelope by the owner or building contractor and agreed on, or it may be simply the selection of a certain standard door or window unit from a catalogue; but in all such cases the job is being designed by someone just as definitively as with a drawing board and T square. The more "someone" knows about the principles of good architectural design, the better the result will be—and therefore much of this book is devoted to taking a detailed look at all parts of the house in order to see how these principles can be applied in real situations and at different budget levels to help toward a better end result.

There are two common misconceptions about design: (a) that it can be applied as a sort of surface treatment at a later stage of the job if there is enough money; (b) that it automatically raises the cost of the job.

The "cosmetic" fallacy—that design is only skin deep and can be applied or not applied according to budget— is responsible for such familiar lapses of taste as fake finishes pretending to be brick, stone, or something else; "original" color schemes visible four blocks away; and all sorts of applied cuteness, used in a vain effort to dress up an intrinsically bad design.

Good design begins with an efficient and attractive internal layout, and follows through with the use of good general shapes and proportions and good detailing of such elements as windows and doors. Needless to say, none of this can be "stuck on"—hence the importance of discussing in detail all these things, tangible and intangible, which make the difference between a good or bad end result.

The other fallacy—that good design always costs more and is therefore a luxury—is believed by many people. The truth is that *good design makes the most of whatever money is available*—whether it be large or small—and is therefore certainly no luxury item. It should also be pointed out that bad or mediocre design is seldom cheap and is often responsible for people wasting money on things that do not contribute to the best total results. In a good rehab design, for example, a few extra dollars may be spent on getting a white or black electrolytically coated, or anodized, window sash instead of a "natural" aluminum one, but that amount may be more than offset by the wise and economical decision to retain and refinish the existing wood balustrade in the inside stairwell instead of "modernizing" it with spidery so-called wrought iron units, which would not belong in such a situation. This book, therefore, will also emphasize the importance of knowing how to use money strategically for the maximum effect, both esthetically and functionally.

It cannot be emphasized too strongly that *good design is good economics from everyone's point of view* and, apart from helping to maintain the long-term value of the individual house, has a very definite effect on the surroundings. Good design by its example can be infectious; on the other hand, it only requires a few pioneers in the nastier forms of rehabilitation and "there goes the neighborhood"—and with it some of the value of each house, good or bad.

For those who want to do the best possible job of rehabilitating an old house but are a little confused by the many possibilities, here are three useful general rules to end this introductory discussion:

1. When in doubt, restore as much of the original as possible—both outside and inside.
2. Never try to make the house seem older than it originally was by using detail of a previous era.
3. If extensive alterations are intended or modern treat-

ments are to be mixed with old, *read this book thoroughly* (and if possible get some direct advice from a good architect).

One last word: Although the design factor may be only a part of the whole process of getting something built, it is of the same importance as the tip of an iceberg, being the part which is normally *seen* and which, to the outside world, *represents the whole.*

II

The Language of Design: General Terms and Principles

Since much of this book will be dealing in some detail with the problems of good design as applied to rehabilitation work, it would be well to say a few words here about some of the terms that have a special meaning in the field of architectural design. Most of the terms—such as proportion, scale, balance, and so forth—are not hard to understand and the reader need have no fear of being snowed under with abstract concepts; they are, however, so important to good design—both new and rehab—that they should really be defined and discussed briefly before being applied.

The first and most basic group of elements with which the designer works consists of *Point, Line, Plane, Mass,* and *Space.* The first two need little explanation: a point theoretically has no size or dimensions and a line only one dimension—length. On a building these might be represented by, say, a doorknob or a small element of projecting decoration and by a thin horizontal projecting band of stone in a brick wall.

With the element *Plane,* another dimension is added,

so that it has both length and width—like a sheet of paper. The planes are the flat surfaces corresponding to the walls, floors, and ceilings of a building and are usually penetrated by such things as windows and doors. Often they are also pushed and pulled around somewhat, or "modeled," for decorative effect, but they are still basically planes. If one part of a wall projects in front of the rest of the wall, as in the case of the front of a bay window, it is said to be on a different plane.

The terms *Mass* and *Space* include a third dimension, so that they have length, width (or height), and depth.

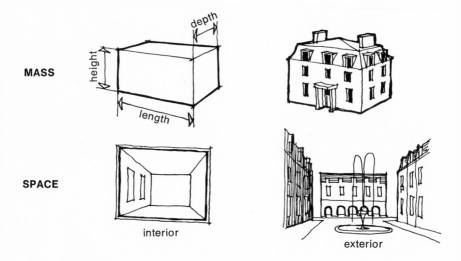

MASS

SPACE

interior

exterior

To put is simply, *Mass* describes the effect of a solid object or box seen from the *outside,* and *Space* the box seen from the *inside* (or literally the air enclosed by the planes of the top, bottom, and sides). A building—particularly a large one—often comprises a number of masses —hence the term *Massing,* which is often used to describe the form of such structures as a cathedral. Likewise, a space can be simple, as in a small box-like room, or compound, as in a Baroque interior of the grand manner, where many different enclosed volumes may interpenetrate and flow into one another (although here the term "spacing" is not used!). Another type of space is the exterior or urban space, which has, of course, no roof but can have an equally strong sense of enclosure from the ground and surrounding buildings, which correspond to the floor and walls of a room—indeed, often the smallest urban squares are the most successful just because of this feeling of secure enclosure.

Needless to say, planes and masses are rarely found in their simplest forms of rectangles and cubes (except in some early pioneering examples of twentieth-century architecture) and this is particularly true of the old buildings being rehabilitated. The gable of a house with a sloping roof, for instance, will not be a square or rectangular plane but more likely a rectangle plus a triangle—also, hopefully, few of the buildings will be literally in the form of a box! In other words, the planes have been given *Shape* and *Contour,* and the masses have been given *Form.*

The decorative elements of *Texture, Pattern, Tone,* and *Color* further modify the planes and surfaces of a building.

Texture is the "touch" quality, or the degree of roughness or smoothness of a material or surface. This ranges from the regular smoothness of glass to the pitted richness of old brickwork, and part of the designer's skill lies in choosing appropriate materials and using them not only in the right place to perform their function, but also so that they blend or contrast effectively and enhance the general design. It is very important that the design be enhanced rather than just "jazzed-up" by the textures, as it is all too easy to use slick materials such as the "natural," or uncoated, aluminum and glass curtain walls, so popular at one time as a commercial rehab panacea, to cover up good honest masonry, or to use inappropriate contrasts such as rustic shingles in an urban street.

Pattern is closely allied to texture and, while not all textures have pattern (i.e., some regularly repeated motif, shape, or form), most patterns have something of the effect of a texture. A smooth wall surface, for instance, will appear less smooth when covered with a pattern. As we shall see later, brickwork has a pattern as well as a texture, and this is sometimes overemphasized by using a mortar that is much lighter or darker than the bricks themselves, making the bricks appear to stand out as units in themselves. These patterns, or "bonds" as they are called, arise directly from the methods of laying bricks to produce walls of different strengths; they are described in Chapter V, page 61. Other such functional patterns (and textures) are formed by the traditional methods of laying other small units, such as slates, tiles, and shingles—and some Victorian slate roofs go even further in using differences in tone, color, and shape to create quite complicated and deliberately "designed" patterns. Needless to say, these should be carefully preserved when possible.

As we see, it is almost impossible to talk about texture and pattern without bringing in *Tone* and *Color*. Texture, tone, and color, especially, are nearly always experienced *together*, whether or not one is aware of them as separate qualities. Texture, in fact, rarely changes without a corresponding change in color and tone—except, perhaps, in the case of the wall of a painted wood Queen Anne house. *Tone*, the least understood of these terms, means simply the relative darkness or lightness of a material or color. This is a property quite distinct from the color itself, and it is possible, for instance, to have both a dark *and* a light tone of red. The effect of tone can best be appreciated by half closing the eyes until most of the color of the house, or anything else, is drained away, leaving only the relative lightness and darkness of the parts. Materials such as traditional red brickwork will then appear darker than, say, concrete or white-painted clapboard.

Strong, natural *Colors* that are relatively unmixed, or "straight-from-the-pot" as it were, tend to have a more-or-less fixed tone value; yellow is the lightest, then green and orange, then blue and red, then blue-violet and purple, and, finally, violet—the naturally darkest color of them all. This can be easily seen by looking at any standard color wheel. Many colors, however, have had their natural tone value changed by intermixture with white, black, or other colors until there is, say, a pale red (or pink) that is actually *lighter* than yellow ochre, producing when seen together a discordant effect that has to be experienced to be believed! Many other colors removed from the natural hierarchy of tone values and used together also tend to form discords which, although they can be used effectively on occasion for sophisticated effects, should generally be avoided—especially outdoors. Dark tones of yellow, for example, tend to look very dirty, and colors based on pale purples and violets are all distinctly shaky propositions for exterior use in other than tropical climates—as shall be seen later when the use of color on exteriors is discussed.

The use of different colors at about the same tone value should also generally be avoided, since it creates a trick optical effect by which the colors seem to advance and recede. This has recently been much exploited in "op art" and can have an exciting effect, but it is definitely not recommended as a day-to-day background for living if one wishes to avoid premature visits to the optometrist or psychiatrist!

The final group of elements could best be described as *Qualities*, which result from the manipulation of the five primary elements of point, line, plane, mass, and space, and are of the utmost importance in determining the general character and design quality of a building. They are: *Proportion, Solid-Void Relationship, Scale, Emphasis, Directional Emphasis, Rhythm, Effect of Light and Shade,* and *Balance.* The names here probably sound more formidable than the ideas they represent—which are really quite simple to grasp once they have been explained (yet another instance of the undesirable, but unfortunately necessary, custom of labeling everything).

Proportion is simply the ratio (or relative size) of two or more dimensions. This can refer to the ratio of the width to the height of a door opening, window opening, or window subdivision or, on a larger scale, to the ratio of the width to the height of a whole building. It can also refer to many other size relationships such as that between the story heights of a house (see page 71).

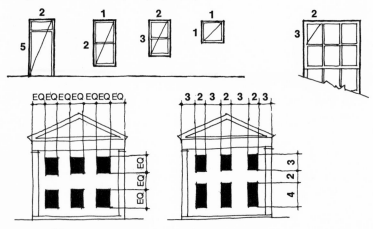

Generally speaking, proportions should be varied and suitably contrasted for greater design interest, the use of the 1:1 ratio being kept to a minimum. In the first of the lower examples above, the fact that all windows and the pieces of wall between them are of the same width and height, tends to give an impression of monotony and, strangely enough, restlessness; in the second example, however, the variation of proportions produces a general effect that is at once more interesting and restful.

Good proportions seldom cost any more than bad proportions and are therefore one of the designer's most effective tools—especially when working within a limited budget.

The *Solid-Void Relationship* is another kind of proportion—that between the total area of solid wall surface and the total area of "holes" (i.e., windows, doors, arches, etc.) of a building. (It should be noted that in the sketch just mentioned, although the windows were equal in *size* to the surrounding pieces of wall, their *total area* did not equal that of the remaining wall surfaces.) The solid-void relationship determines the appearance of a building in a very basic way, with a range of possibilities extending from the fortress to the glass house.

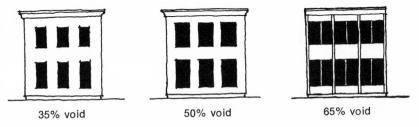

35% void   50% void   65% void

Above are three different treatments of similar buildings. In the first sketch the wall dominates, obviously supporting the building, and is pierced only by such windows as are necessary to admit adequate light to the interior; this is a normal, traditional approach, and the effect, generally, is orderly and restful. In the second sketch the total area of the windows has been increased until it is about equal to that of the surrounding wall (the dreaded 1:1 ratio!), and the general effect tends to be rather restless and less satisfactory. This effect occurs because the wall has been largely destroyed as a unity and now appears only as a series of bands between the windows; furthermore, it may no longer actually be capable of supporting the building, the real work being done by columns or piers behind the scene. In this case the treatment shown in Figure 3 would be a more honest expression of what is going on, structurally speaking, while at the same time achieving a more restful balance of solid-to-void, this time with the "void," or glass, dominating.

The more-glass-than-wall situation is, of course, rarely seen in older houses—other than in conservatory extensions —and is more often found in commercial or public buildings, most particularly in those built during this century. In certain houses where the *width* of the windows exceeds that of the wall between them, however, it will not be possible to install proper exterior blinds or shutters—as we shall see later.

Scale is yet another form of proportion—this time expressed as the relationship of the *apparent* size of a building, space, or object to the size of a human being; a "large" scale, as in a public building, will tend to impress the viewer, whereas a smaller scale, more suitable for dwellings, will be more human and friendly, and so on. The word "apparent" is stressed because buildings can be made to seem larger or smaller than they actually are by changing their appearance of scale.

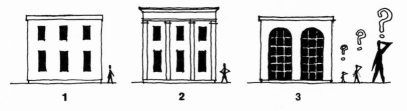

In the first example above the windows at once establish the size of the building and tell us that it is two-storied. In the second example the windows still clearly relate to the size of a human being but the scale of the building has been altered, and its effect made more imposing by the use of giant two-story columns such as are found in Greek Revival houses. In each of these cases one would have no difficulty if asked to sketch a person alongside the building at approximately the correct relative size. In Figure 3, however, this would not be easy. Here all details that could be related to the human figure have been removed and the sense of scale has been lost: one could be looking at anything from a humble bus shelter to a multi-story factory! The surroundings, such as people, trees, and cars, would at once, of course, reveal the true size of the building—but it is an important architectural principle that *a building must establish its own scale* without outside aids. (NOTE: *Scale* has also a technical meaning, for which see glossary.)

The use of suitably placed *Emphasis* is one of the ways of avoiding over-all monotony in a building that may otherwise be well designed, with good proportions and a good sense of scale.

The somewhat bland front shown in Figure 1 above has been livened in the second illustration by emphasizing the doorway with a porch. Misplaced emphasis, however, which draws attention to something relatively unimportant in an attempt to "liven things up," should be avoided. Color, for instance, which is an important means of emphasis, is often misused in this way, extra-strong colors being employed to give an inappropriate amount of importance to such items as shutters, roofs, and so forth.

The *Directional Emphasis* of a building is one of its most important characteristics, and, with very few exceptions, most of the older buildings eligible for rehabilitation will be predominantly vertical in character—at least in the most important details such as windows, bay projections, and so forth. This is important to remember when making any alterations or additions to the original design—and *most particularly when new or existing windows are involved in any way.*

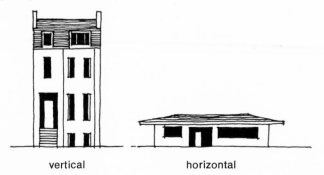

vertical   horizontal

Rhythm is another device that helps avoid monotony, particularly in long buildings or streets. If, for instance, the simple front used here to illustrate emphasis were to be repeated ad infinitum as a street front, a sort of waltz rhythm would result, each house representing the three-beats-to-the-measure and the doorways the heavy down-beat, i.e., DOOR-window-window, DOOR-window-window.

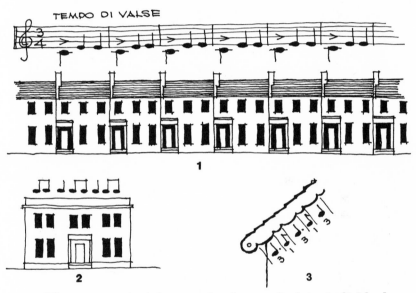

The same principle can also be applied to individual buildings by the use, say, of some regularly repeated pattern of proportions, as in Figure 2—which is of a rather large building, needless to say. In the average house, however, rhythm is usually seen on a considerably smaller scale, such as in the fretted "bargeboards"—a typical example of which is illustrated in Figure 3—that appear on the gables of many Gothic Revival houses.

The *Effect of Light and Shade* is another way of adding to the interest of an architectural design, by using projections and recessions that both catch the light and cast shadows. It emphasizes the third dimension of *depth* and often gives life to an otherwise "flat" composition.

Textures and patterns are often stressed by the use of light and shade, as in brick and clapboard walls, where fine shadows and light-struck edges enhance the general effect when seen in certain lights.

The last element that must be defined is one of the most important of all—*Balance*. This, or the lack of it, is one of the elements one notices most—consciously or unconsciously—when first looking at a building, and it is not too much to say that if balance is lacking, the building will never be a fully satisfactory design, however well the other elements have been handled. Pages could be written on the subject, exploring its many aspects and subtleties, but for the present purposes the following diagrams may help to summarize the basic essentials.

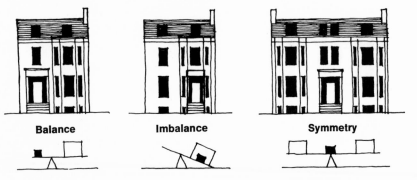

| Balance | Imbalance | Symmetry |

The first two sketches are of a simple house front with two principal features, a porch and a vertical bay with windows, arranged in two different ways, and underneath each is a diagram attempting to show the equivalent effect in terms of actual weights placed on a "see-saw" balance. For this purpose the entrance with its porch has been thought of as the equivalent of a small but heavy weight and the three-story bay as a larger but relatively lighter one. In Figure 1, as in many typical house fronts, the weights balance each other, but in Figure 2, placing the entrance on the other side completely upsets the balance.

One of the traditional methods of achieving balance is by *Symmetry*, illustrated separately in Figure 3. Here, a sense of effort or movement apparent in Figure 1—caused by the balance being achieved *in spite of differences* in the parts—has given place to the effortlessness of an essentially static type of balance, which has long been associated with monuments and the quality of "monumentality." Many design problems arise from the careless mixing of symmetrical and nonsymmetrical elements. In a symmetrical house, for instance, the doorway will be in the center and should be *symmetrical in itself*, being flanked by equal sidelights if there are any. In an asymmetrical house, on the other hand, the door unit will most likely be located to one side and may, or may not, be symmetrical in itself—depending on its immediate surroundings. Symmetry will be touched on again in Chapter VI when discussing entrances, doors, and porches.

The above are the basic elements and principles with which the architectural designer works. At this point some readers may be wondering why it is so important to know about the possible choices on the application of these elements when in the average rehabilitation job they have already been largely determined by the original designer of the house. It is important because the person who knows something about the basic elements of architectural design is in a better position to appreciate how the original design character of a house was formed and therefore to respect and preserve the best of it when making any alterations—however seemingly small.

III

Some Preliminaries: Selecting and Financing a House; Choosing an Architect and/or Builder

Before any actual rehabilitation work can take place there are certain preliminary steps that usually have to be gone through, such as selecting a house if necessary, discovering the best ways of financing a loan, choosing the right architect if one is being used, and finding a good builder who will be sympathetic to one's aims and requirements. There is not enough space here to go into great detail on these matters—some of which have already been adequately dealt with in other books—but it might be appropriate to begin with some "capsule" advice for those who are doing all this for the first time and need information (or perhaps reassurance) rather urgently.

Homeowners will avoid many of the pitfalls that lead to trouble, frustration, and eventual disillusionment if they know a little about the general process of getting something built—however small it may be—and are aware of their relationship to the other parties involved, such as the architect or builder. This must include, of course, an awareness of their obligations as well as their rights: once a contract has been signed, for instance, an owner should restrain himself from making frequent or extensive changes in the work if he wants to remain on friendly terms with the other parties and avoid getting stuck with a substantial bill for all the extras at the end of the job! Additional charges are by far the most common cause of dissatisfaction. There is a well-known story about a famous architect who once advised a client, who had been making almost daily changes on the job, to save himself money by taking a six-month vacation overseas . . . How many architects and builders on smaller jobs must wish that they could say the same!

Putting first things first, however, we will start with a few words of guidance for those who have not yet bought a house and are still in the process of looking for one with good rehabilitation potential.

Selecting a House

Choosing a house can be almost like choosing clothes: so many of the factors involved are purely personal, arising from individual preferences and prejudices, that it may seem a little presumptuous to try to tell anyone what to do. Like clothes, houses tend to be an expression of personalities (by accident if not by design), and many of the older houses present a unique opportunity at moderate cost to indulge in a taste for spacious interiors and meandering room layouts, or to revel in riots of rooftops studded with gables, dormers, and turrets. And why not? . . . provided, of course, that one knows exactly what one is buying in terms of personal livability and potential maintenance.

Most of the cautions offered here, therefore, will be confined to elements that could prove to be major maintenance problems or that might detract seriously from the livability of a house.

Before buying a house with the intention of rehabilitating it, it is always wise to have it looked at by a good architect or builder. If the mortgage loan for the purchase of the house is being provided by the federal government or a bank

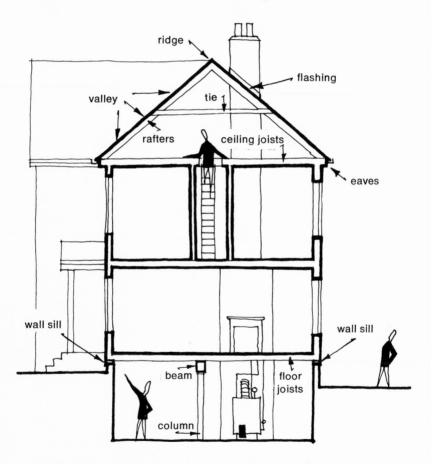

Places To Look When Inspecting a House

they will, of course, arrange to have the property surveyed in order to safeguard themselves, but such surveys are usually confined to the *condition* of the building and do not take into account such things as its suitability for the particular needs of the buyer or such probable maintenance expenses as high heating bills or leak-prone roofs. A good architect or builder, on the other hand, will not only alert the buyer to any such problems but will also be in a position to give him a rough estimate of the total cost of rehabilitation.

For present purposes, however, we will assume that the reader is making his own initial survey, having selected a house and a neighborhood.

The first thing to do is to take a good over-all look at the house from both outside and inside. This may reveal some of the more obvious faults such as unequal settlement of the walls, which will show up in the form of general distortion and, in the case of masonary walls, vertical or zigzag cracks. Lintels and sills that are not horizontal and windows and doors that do not fit their frames often point to this condition.

The main enemy of an old house, however, is water and dampness, so after making a general "eyeball" survey of the property, one should concentrate one's attention on certain areas that are principally so affected and that are readily visible without having to tear away plaster or poke holes in someone else's wall.

The basement, if there is one, is an excellent place to begin, since it is easily accessible and can reveal much of what is going on "behind the scenes." Look first for signs of excessive dampness or recent flooding and, if there are some, try to find out how often such flooding occurs and how bad it is. Don't just take the present owner's or the agent's word for this, either—talk quietly with some of the neighbors, too, for if there is a flooding problem the expense of installing a pump will probably have to be added to your list. Next look carefully at all exposed woodwork, such as the beams of the floor above, the supporting columns, and so forth, to see if it is in sound condition. If there are holes with what appears to be sawdust near them they may be the work of termites or other destructive insects, and if the wood comes away like dry cork when a pen knife is applied, professional advice should be sought. Likewise, if there are areas of damp fungus-like stains on the wood they are likely the result of so-called dry rot, and expert advice will again be necessary. Rot can of course be halted, but this will depend on just how far it has gone and how much strength has been taken out of the timbers.

In a timber frame house the wooden outer wall usually rests on a masonry foundation wall rising the full height of the basement, and where they meet there is a long horizontal wooden piece known as the sill. It is usually around the level of the bottom of the overhead beams in the basement, and since it is the base of the wooden part of the outer wall, any water coming down through that wall will generally end up there. By inspecting the wall sill, therefore, one can get a good idea of the location of certain major leaks in the outer wall.

While in the basement one should also take a good look at the condition of the furnace, the electrical wiring, and the water supply and drainage pipes—all potential maintenance items. If most of the pipes are of copper this is a good indication that the plumbing is relatively new and most likely in good condition. Any lead pipes, on the other hand, have probably been there since the house was built and most likely will have to be replaced. Electrical services are more difficult to generalize on, since what might be safe, legal, and perfectly adequate for one owner may not be for another. Electrical stoves and clothes dryers, for instance, run on 220 volts—twice as much as for other appliances—and if the previous owner has not used them, a special service may have to be installed at a cost. Overloading electrical wiring is like trying to force a large quantity of water through too thin a pipe—except that when it bursts it results in a potentially dangerous burn-out instead of just a messy flood. Generally speaking, therefore, if there is to be any significant change in the life styles of the house-owners, it will be necessary to have the electrical services thoroughly checked to prevent possible overloading.

The other part of the house where one can most readily see behind the scenes is the attic or roof space, and every effort should be made to get up there—particularly if there are any signs of dampness in the walls or partitions of the house. If the roof is in need of total repair that fact will probably have been obvious from the ground outside, but otherwise a visit to the inside of the roof may often disclose leaks that are less readily seen but are rotting the timbers. This wood rot—the "dry rot" already referred to—is actually a fungus and thrives on a combination of dampness and lack of ventilation; therefore, if a leaky roof space is not ventilated, it can form an ideal breeding ground. (Oddly enough, for this reason houses that have been abandoned are sometimes less affected by wood rot if they have been ventilated by a few broken windows!) The places in the roof most vulnerable to leaks are the eaves (the lowest part of the roof), the metal flashing at the point where the roof runs into a chimney or a parapet wall, and those areas where the roof changes plane, such as at a ridge or a valley. If excessive moisture has been penetrating the roof it may also have gone down into the walls or partitions to cause rot, and any suspected area should be probed or uncovered to make absolutely sure that it is sound.

If an outer wall is being opened up, this is a good chance to see if there is any form of insulation inside. One should also look in the attic, since a total absence of insulation—particularly in the roof—can mean several hundred extra dollars on the heating bill each year.

When looking at walls and partitions from inside the house it is also wise to look for long cracks in the plaster and for doors and windows that do not fit squarely in their frames. These are all symptoms of unequal settlement in the foundations or frame and may warrant some further inspection. The deformed windows will, of course, already have shown up on the outside, but if there is any doubt about their condition it can be further confirmed by actually opening (or trying to open) them.

Finding Out About Loans

While looking for a house the prospective buyer should give some thought as to how he wants to finance the purchase. There are a number of ways in which those who are either buying or rehabilitating a house—or doing both—can go about this, the most common being by means of a loan from the bank or from the federal or state government. The interest rates on these alternatives may vary considerably, so if the owner does not want to pay more than necessary for his loan (and who does?) it is to his advantage to find out about all the possibilities open to him before making a final decision. This advice applies particularly if the house is within the boundaries of such areas as Urban Renewal or Model Cities projects, where federal loans at specially low rates, as well as certain grants, may be available for the purpose of bringing the property at least up to the minimum requirements of the local building code.

Such grants and loans vary according to time and place, however; therefore contact the nearest federal and state housing offices (i.e., HUD, FHA, State Planning Department) to see what is available before going to a bank.

Selecting the Architect

Some of the advantages of having the services of a good architect have already been mentioned. However, if the reader does not want, or feels that he cannot afford, an architect he should read this section anyway, since he may find himself in the position of having to perform some of the duties himself.

Most people are somewhat flabbergasted when confronted with the problem of choosing an architect. Like other professions, that of architecture contains a wide variety of talent and competence and the homeowner naturally wants to get the best for his money. How then to go about it?

It has been said often by the cynics that whereas doctors bury their mistakes, architects make monuments of them . . . Although this, fortunately, is not generally true, architects do have to make a visible show of their competence sooner or later in some tangible form and, as one lecturer in an architectural school once rather ominously put it, "People will be within a stone's throw of your buildings." This, then, is the key to finding an architect: simply look around for rehabilitation work of a type and design quality that you admire, find out who the architect is, and go to see him. If there is no good domestic rehab around, look for good commercial work, for an architect who has made a good job of bringing out the best of an older building for, say, a bank or an office, can be expected to do the same with a house. The architect will gladly show you other examples of his work both in reality and photographic form and should have no objection, for instance, if you wanted to talk to some of his clients to get their opinions of his work. (Check any adverse criticism afterwards with the architect to find out if in fact it was his fault.)

Selecting an architect for rehabilitation work may take a little longer than selecting one for new work, since it is somewhat of a specialization and many otherwise good— even brilliant—members of the profession have been conspicuously unsuccessful in relating their work to buildings of other eras. In addition to imagination and technical competence, it may take a certain humility and readiness to submerge one's own ego as a designer to bring out the best in an old building—and these qualities are not always forthcoming from that architect who is mainly interested in leaving his own personal mark on the world. There are plenty of excellent architects, however, who do *not* fall into this category, and if one keeps an eye out for unassuming work done with style, they won't be hard to find.

When choosing an architect it is important to know exactly what services he can offer. These are much more extensive than most people realize.

The most important function of the architect is to act as the agent of the owner to see that the work is designed and built properly. The actual extent of his services will vary widely according to the size and nature of the job, but for the purpose of completeness, here is a list of some services he would be expected to perform for a new building or for a large rehabilitation job:

1. THE DESIGN STAGE. Measuring the existing building (in the case of a rehab job) and drawing up an accurate record of existing conditions; designing and drawing the new plans or layouts and the elevations (or what the building will look like from outside), also any sections or cuts necessary to show changes being made to the inside and any perspectives or sketches necessary to show what the outside or parts of the inside will look like when seen from given points. Perspectives are not always required, of course, but can be useful both for convincing the owner that he is doing the right thing and for inspiring the bank to lend him the money to do it.

2. THE WORKING DRAWING AND SPECIFICATION STAGE. Working drawings are a set of accurate and fully dimensioned drawings from which the builder will perform the work, and specifications are a written description of the materials and methods to be used. These, with the formal contract, constitute a legal agreement from which neither the builder, the architect, nor the owner can depart without the consent of the other parties and an appropriate readjustment of the agreed total price of the job. These documents are a safeguard for the owner against being short-changed and for the builder against over-frequent and unreasonable demands for changes on the job.

3. SUPERVISION OF THE JOB. If no builder has been selected, it may at this stage be part of the archi-

tect's duties to organize the bidding for the job among three or more builders, and to advise the owner in selecting the best offer. Alternately, the job may be given directly to a builder of the owner's choice in the form of a negotiated contract, under which a single builder is authorized to execute the project according to the owner's wishes, usually within a stipulated price limit. Here the experience of the architect can be invaluable in making this crucial selection. Once the job starts, the architect will act on behalf of the owner, making visits to the job as often as necessary to see that the work is being executed properly, and he will also act as liaison between the builder and the owner when problems arise.

In addition to all these services the architect will hire such consultants as are necessary for excavation and soil, structural, heating, and electrical engineering and, a fact not generally known, pay them out of his own fee.

For full services such as described an architect would base his fee on a percentage of the cost of construction, varying from ten to fifteen percent, as laid down by the American Institute of Architects. Most rehabilitation jobs, however, do not require all these services—particularly those of the consultant engineers—and so it is often best all around (and less expensive for the owner) for the architect himself to be hired as a consultant on an hourly basis. In such cases it is customary for the architect to state in writing to the owner his precise charge per hour for the various skills involved (i.e., partners' time, drafting time, etc.) a projected ceiling figure for the total architectural work beyond which it cannot go without the owner's approval. This is known as the Letter of Acceptance and a copy should be signed by the owner and returned to the architect, thereby authorizing him to proceed with the work.

At his request, the owner can be billed periodically as an indication of how the work is proceeding. Usually a small retaining fee is appreciated by most architects (and required by some) before putting pencil to paper, as an act of good faith.

Selecting the Builder

If the owner decides that he does not require the services of an architect he will have to make the vital decision of choosing the builder himself. This choice is probably the most important one he will make, since there will be no architect around to act as his watchdog on quality and performance when the job begins. Again, however, there are plenty of competent and honest builders around, and the owner's problem is how to be sure the one he selects belongs to this category. The direct recommendation of someone whose judgement is trusted may be a good point of departure—providing that some fair samples of the builder's work can actually be seen. Otherwise the local bank, hardware store, or lumberyard will usually be able to come up with the names of some local builders of good repute whose work can also be inspected. In each case a talk with some of the past clients might also be helpful.

As well as being competent, the builder should be familiar with, and sympathetic to, the type of design approach and finishes required; otherwise the end result may be quite different from what *seemed* to be agreed on at the signing of the contract. Someone who is trying to keep as many of the original features of his house as his pocket will permit, for instance, is not likely to be happy with a builder who is a rigid adherent of the Cheaper-to-Rip-It-All-Off approach. On the other hand, the homeowner should not blame the builder if what he requires is really impossible at the price he is prepared to pay, for some of the problems of rehabilitation can only be solved at considerable expense. This may all sound a bit depressing, but after talking to a few builders the owner will be in a better position to judge for himself which one is best suited to the job and exactly how far it may be necessary to modify his original ideas to fit in with the budget. As in many other areas, some negotiation is a crucial part of doing anything worthwhile well.

Sometimes the best way of finding the right builder is to use the same technique that we described for finding an architect—simply look around for examples of good work of a similar type to what you have in mind and talk with the owners to find out who the builders were.

The next decision to be made is whether the builder is to act as general contractor, organizing all the trades involved (i.e., bricklayer, carpenter, plumber, electrician, etc.), or whether the owner wants to do this himself and sub-contract each trade directly. The latter course is usually inadvisable unless:

1. the job is quite small; OR
2. the owner knows something of the capabilities of the sub-contractors; AND
3. the owner has enough time at his disposal to plan the phasing-in of each trade and to be readily available *on the job* as problems arise within or between the trades.

Bad coordination between the trades can hold up the progress of the job for weeks, so the time factor may also enter into the picture. It is generally better, therefore, and often cheaper in the long run (if one has to take paid time off other work) to let the chosen builder act as general contractor for the whole job.

If there is no strongly favored contractor, it is customary to take bids for the work from several and to compare them. It is essential here, however, to know *exactly* what each one is bidding on and to be aware of any differences which will affect the prices, since *the lowest price may not always be the best bargain.*

When one reaches the point of signing the contract with the builder it is also most important to see that the extent and details of the job are properly covered in the contract specifications and/or drawings. This is essential for the protection of both parties, as previously mentioned.

At some time before the contract is signed, the owner should check with the local Building Department to see if the proposed work will be in violation of the local building code and to find out what sort of drawings may be required to obtain a building permit. This will also give him a little time to apply for any variance needed if the building or zoning codes are being violated in any way. Later it is customary for the builder to "walk" any necessary drawings through the Department when he applies for his building permit; in the meantime, someone must prepare these drawings, and for those who intend to do it themselves for a simple rehab job, the essentials will be discussed in a later chapter.

Some of the Styles Commonly Used in Nineteenth-Century Houses

These examples represent five of the most popular "revival" styles found in many parts of America. The approximate date of the earliest introduction of each style has been given, and allowance should be made for certain time lags that may have occurred before it was adopted in different areas of the country.

Single, detached houses have been selected for the illustrations only because they tend to show more of the characteristic details of each style; the remarks, however, apply equally to combined and row houses. Needless to say, *all* of the details will not be found in *every* example of the style and there are also many other details that it has not been possible to include.

It should be noted that architectural historians tend to classify buildings by the style of the *detail* rather than the general shape—sometimes with rather strange results. Thus, a row house which in nearly every respect resembles the English Georgian prototype may actually be classified as Greek Revival because of two Doric columns at the doorway! When in doubt, therefore, look at the details.

The buildings shown here are also often referred to as "Victorian"—but this denotes the *era* in which they were built rather than their style.

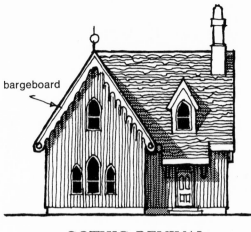

bargeboard

GOTHIC REVIVAL
(from 1830)

This is one of the easiest styles to identify, although the individual examples may be the most difficult to put dates to. This is because it remained in use for the greater part of the century—unlike the other styles, which were fashionable only for twenty to thirty years each. To many it typifies Victorianism with its love of "busy" details and picturesque fussiness (which on occasion was carried to excess) and because of this is often referred to by such affectionate names as the Gingerbread Style.

The style is loosely based on some of the characteristics of medieval Gothic church architecture and, although principally identified with churches and public buildings, the style—or at least the detail associated with the style—is also found in many of the most charming houses of the period, the relative scarcity of examples giving it extra value.

Characteristics and Details: Emphasis on verticality, steeply sloping roofs, details that tend to hang down or stand up, pointed windows, conspicuous gables—often with elaborately decorated bargeboards and eaves.

45

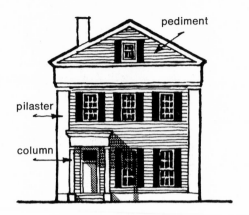

GREEK REVIVAL
(from 1830)

This style was widely popular in the second quarter of the nineteenth century and was inspired by the reawakening of interest in ancient Greek architecture, a result of the discoveries of the new science of archeology. The temple was regarded as the ideal form, so not only banks and civic buildings but also houses tended to be turned "end on" as it were so that the gable could be treated in a manner approximating that of the main front of the Parthenon and other acknowledged Greek masterpieces.

Characteristics and Details: Comparatively low sloping roofs that form, with the main entablature, a strongly triangulated pediment (see above) which in turn rests on columns or on pilasters, flat columns embedded in a wall. Columns are modeled on the original Greek "orders" (see glossary) and not on the Roman versions, which are seen in other classical revival styles. Windows tend to be tall with "six-over-six" subdivisions.

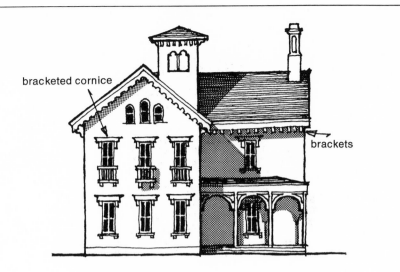

bracketed cornice

brackets

ITALIANATE or BRACKETED
(from 1845)

Also known as the Italian Villa style, this represents a return to the picturesque after the relatively simple classical lines of Greek Revival. The style is based not so much on the examples of the high Renaissance as on their provincial Italian farmhouse adaptations, sometimes with more than a hint of Gothic "busyness" thrown in.

Characteristics and Details: The general appearance is of an asymmetrical but balanced composition of gables, roofs, porches, etc.—usually with a square tower capped by a low-piched roof as a prominent feature. The characteristic brackets under the eaves are emphasized by the broad projection of the roofs. Balconies, bay windows, and double round-headed windows are typical of the style, as is the use of bracketed cornices and bracketed sills at the windows.

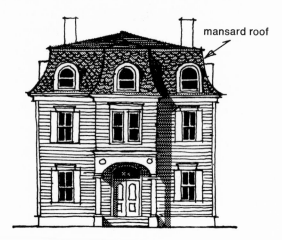

mansard roof

MANSARD or FRENCH
SECOND EMPIRE
(from 1855)

This style is named after, and easily identified by, the mansard roof, which is its most prominent characteristic; this type of roof has two slopes on all four sides (see "roof types" in glossary). The style came directly from France, where it was popular about the same time—hence its other name, Second Empire.

Characteristics and Details: Mansard roof with dormer windows *always.* "Two-over-two" window subdivisions. Half-round slates often used in steeper slope of the roof. Sometimes the upper slope of roof may be so slight as to be invisible from ground level.

pent roof

cut-away corner

QUEEN ANNE
(from 1880)

This style is another "picturesque" reaction to classicism as represented by the Second Empire. The name is thoroughly misleading, being the American version of a very free popular contemporary English style that in reality owed practically nothing to the earlier architecture associated with the reign of Queen Anne.

Characteristics and Details: A general preoccupation with the picturesque (and almost medieval) arrangement of roofs, dormers, chimneys, and gables—the gables often forming right-angled triangles with the aid of a cornice or pent roof (see drawing). The use of different textures or materials on the same wall. Cutaway corners with windows. Occasional use of "six-over-one" window subdivisions.

IV

The Exterior: General Considerations

Although much rehabilitation work is confined to the interior of buildings—or tends to proceed from the inside outward as it were—the exterior will be dealt with first so that certain important general aspects of rehabilitation can be discussed. Also, for those who are looking for (or just *at*) houses, it is the exterior that usually makes the first—and often the most lasting—impression, which tends to form pro or con prejudices even before the inside is seen. It is not generally recommended to make the first visit after dark, but in some cases it might lead to a fairer judgment; perhaps the ideal would be to enter the house blindfolded and to look at the outside afterward—if you don't care what your potential neighbors think! At all events the prospective buyer should no more judge a house than a person by first external impressions, for, as everyone knows, those whose faults are mainly on the surface often prove in the long run to be easier to live with . . .

The outside of the house forms a large part of the visible tip of the rehabilitation "iceberg" already referred to, and it is certainly fair to say that what one does there will affect more people than what one does to the inside. In other words, mistakes in interior layout may be a private tragedy, but a badly designed exterior can be a public disaster!

Although not always in the category of "disasters," the exterior results produced by many well-intentioned persons are often mediocre or bad, both by architectural design and neighborhood-improvement standards. Sometimes this is blamed on lack of money, but it has been the author's experience that bad design is not limited to any income bracket, and that poor expensive and medium-priced design is in every way as common as poor low-priced design. Rather than lack of money it is usually lack of knowledge of how to use money to best advantage that spoils much rehabilitation work. This knowledge can only come about through an awareness of the basic principles of architectural design, discussed in the last chapter, and—still more important—*the ability to apply it in everyday situations.* Much of the balance of this book, therefore, will be devoted to just this problem: relating simple design theory to practical rehabilitation work, with a special emphasis on the selection of standard manufactured parts.

Hopefully, this will enable those who are genuinely interested in doing the right thing by an old house but are unsure of themselves to get a clearer idea not only of *what* to do, but *why.*

The House and the Environment

Just as "no man is an island," a house also owes something to the street and neighborhood to which it belongs (or the "environment" as the planners like to call it). This is known as architectural good manners and was at certain times in the past accepted without question as a part of social good manners. In this century, however, good manners—both architectural and social—have taken a drop in prestige, and the environment may be menaced both by the self-centered man who feels it is no one else's concern what his building looks like and the muscle-flexing architect who values conspicuous originality and self-expression above all other qualities—an unholy alliance! (Some architects still do not seriously bother to relate their work to the existing surroundings on the theory that all older buildings are obsolete and will soon be replaced by new ones, which will, of course, match their own . . .) The cold realities of ecology and the revival of interest in the city as a historical growth have now made both the "home is my castle" and the "divine right of the creator" philosophies quite obsolete, but their influence, unfortunately, is still strong. In the commercial world the temptation to "modernize" by the excessive use of "natural" aluminum and gaudy colored panels is still too much for many store owners and this, combined with oversized commercial signs of nasty design have largely ruined the character of Main Street, Anywhere.

In the rehabilitation of houses, the results on the whole have not been quite so drastic, but some of the standardized parts and materials we have mentioned in passing have done quite a thorough job of de-characterizing and confusing many houses and neighborhoods that once had charm. In place of genuine clapboard, for instance, one now finds artificial brickwork or stonework (to say nothing of real brickwork and stonework that might as well be plastic) and instead of—or in front of—the original doors there is perhaps an aluminum caricature of a "Colonial" door (complete with stamped-on "woodwork," dummy hinges, and frills), that owes more to Hans Christian Andersen than American history—to name but a few of the familiar details! Such things are sold widely in the name of "home improvement" and will be discussed in greater detail in the next chapter; their influence has been of such magnitude, however, that it is important to say a few words about them right now before going on.

Today, to an extent never before in history, there are standard ready-made products available to replace just about every part of a house, whether old or new. This is both good and bad. While making it much easier to make an old house warm or water-tight—something certainly not to be undervalued—it also makes it possible to change the appearance of the house radically (even when this is not intended) simply by quoting a few catalogue numbers. If most of the available products were of good design—as in Sweden, for instance—this might not matter so greatly, but as things are, the buyer is faced by a frighteningly large choice of items to put onto or into his house—all claiming to "modernize" or "improve" it—most of which are of mediocre to bad design by any reasonable architectural standard. Unfortunately, many of the most convenient and easily obtainable items—such as some of the most commonly used doors and windows—fall into this category and have had the effect of standardizing bad design.

In the manufacture of building accessories, "know-how" seems to have far outdistanced "know-why," and many products have appeared on the market not because they were really needed, but simply because *it was technically possible to make them.* Furthermore, there seems to be a current fascination in mimicry for its own sake, to judge by the myriad fake materials which are available. For these reasons alone it would seem to make a lot of sense if, in the interest of our total environment, manufacturers and architects could somehow get together in an honest effort to try to improve the general design standard of building parts.

The picture is not totally dark, however, and there are plenty of fine, well-designed products available on the market for those who have the knowledge or the patience to hunt them out. The architectural profession itself has been profoundly affected by the growing necessity for "design by selection," and two of the most important adjuncts of any good office are now the library of manufacturers' catalogues and the sample room, which has everything from small chips of colored plastic to real windows (or reduced versions of them). Needless to say, the amateur does not have these resources and will not usually be in a position, through previous experience, to have performance records of a particular material; he can, however, do his own research and reduce the bewildering extent of possible choices by becoming conversant with the qualities of good design —for, fortunately, what is well designed is often well made.

Good manners in architecture do not require that all buildings on a street look alike or even be in the same style, any more than social good manners require everyone to wear a gray suit, and there is still plenty of scope for variety in design and in the selection of manufactured parts. They do require, however, that each building has a relationship to its neighbors, and this may take the form either of harmony, contrast, or, quite likely, a mixture of both. Thus, a neighborly house may harmonize with the surrounding architecture in scale, size, and general proportion and yet contrast with it in the treatment of details such as windows and doors—if they are appropriate to the building and of good design.

54

In certain unique historic districts, where it is essential not to harm the character of the environment, efforts have been made to find out just what it is that makes a building "belong" to the area for the guidance of those intending to put up new buildings there. In Savannah, Georgia, for instance, a system of points has been developed for assessing the compatability of a proposed structure with the local surroundings: sixteen ways are identified in which the building can relate to its neighbors and it must conform to at least six of these before it is considered acceptable. These criteria have been attractively and clearly illustrated in a brochure and are reproduced in Appendix A by permission of Historic Savannah, Inc. Although these criteria were intended for a specific historic urban area, most of the points are generally valid elsewhere and could form an excellent basis for arriving at some idea of archtectural compatability in the average neighborhood—both urban and suburban. Although they may not automatically produce good design, they would, if applied, go a long way toward eliminating the more obvious eyesores commonly found almost everywhere.

When rehabilitating an existing house, some of the ways in which it can relate itself to the street or neighborhood are, of course, already decided—such as its height, the main proportions, and its relationship to the street—and there is little that one can do about them even if one wanted to, short of extensive alterations or actually moving the structure. Some of the other ways, however, such as relationship of materials, texture, color, and detailing, are nearly always the subject of choice, and a modified list for rehabilitation work in a neighborhood that has retained some of its original character might read as follows:

Basic ways in which a remodeled exterior can relate itself to the street or neighborhood

GENERAL WAYS:

1. By relating the materials to those predominant in the area, i.e., brick, clapboard, etc.
2. By relating the textures to those predominant in the area, i.e., rough brickwork, closely spaced clapboards, etc.
3. By relating the colors to those predominant in the area, i.e., traditional red brickwork, white clapboards, etc.
4. By relating the details to those predominant in the area, i.e., type of door and window trim, cornices, lintels, arches, chimneys, ironwork, and so forth.

IF MORE EXTENSIVE ALTERATIONS ARE INTENDED:

5. By the proportion of the openings, i.e., the width-to-height relationship of windows and doors (see page 22).
6. By the proportion of the *area* of the openings to the *area* of surrounding wall, i.e., the "openness" (see pages 23–4).

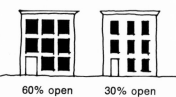

60% open   30% open

7. By the rhythm of solid-to-void, i.e., a repeating relationship of the width of the doors and windows to the width of wall between (see page 27).
8. By adherence to any general rhythm that may be set up in the street or neighborhood by the repetition of such elements as bay windows, entrances, porches, or stair projections; this applies

particularly to streets of row houses (see page 27).

9. By the relationship of the roof shapes to those predominant in the area, i.e., flat, high pitch, low pitch, gable, hipped, gambrel, or mansard (see glossary).

10. By the scale, i.e., the *apparent* size of a building in relationship to a man—"large scale," "small scale," etc. (see page 24).

11. By the directional expression, i.e., the combined effect of the proportions of the openings and of the building itself, which will give a general effect either of verticality or horizontality; most nineteenth-century houses are predominantly vertical in effect (see page 26).

12. By the use of certain site or landscape features predominant in the area, i.e., brick walls, freestone walls, cobble paving, and so forth.

These criteria are put forward as suggestions and may not all carry equal weight in all neighborhoods. On the whole, the first four are probably the most important in establishing basic character. In the rehabilitation of an existing house, meeting a minimum of six out of these twelve would be quite reasonable, providing that the choice included two out of the first four. The main purpose of this list, however, is for use by the reader as a checklist, for as a general rule the more ways his house can identify itself with the neighborhood—without losing its own character—the better.

So much for houses in neighborhoods that have retained some of their original character. The person whose house is not so fortunately situated, however, may well be asking what he should do in an area, say, that has literally been "covered" by salesmen of some of the more objectionable synthetic sidings already mentioned. The answer is simple: first try to relate to any desirable qualities that may be left in the surroundings and then let the original character of the house itself be the guide.

V

The Exterior: Choosing Materials and Colors

Choosing Materials

As seen from the list of design criteria, the choice of materials, textures, and colors is among the most important decisions in establishing the basic character of the house, and, in fact, more rehabilitation jobs are spoiled by the use of inappropriate and fake materials than for any other reason. With the hundreds of products available on the market, selection—as already noted—becomes difficult, so a few basic rules might help in the process of elimination.

For the purpose of rehabilitation, building materials and parts can be divided into three categories:

1. Those suitable for use when trying to preserve or enhance the appearance of an old house.
2. Those suitable for use when the house is being modified to permit certain modern treatments.
3. Those which are of neither genuine traditional nor good modern design *and which should be avoided in all situations.*

In the first category there are, of course, all the traditional materials, such as brick, stone, wood, clapboard, slate, and tile, and, because of the difficulty and expense of obtaining the last two items, asphalt shingles should be included, which match them in color. In category two—acceptable modern materials—there can be added to the above such items as vinyl and aluminum siding, black, white, or bronze-colored metal windows and doorframes of appropriate design, flush doors (i.e., doors with one continuous flat surface instead of paneling or glass), and single-paned glazed doors (i.e., doors consisting of one large single pane of glass surrounded by a simple flat wood or metal frame). The doors in each case may be finished in natural or stained wood or can be painted. Category three —unacceptable materials—which has already been discussed, is unfortunately a very large one and includes such items as artificial brick, artificial stone, asbestos wall shingles, pastel-colored roof shingles, and the legion of parts and accessories mainly connected with doors and windows that are generally characterized by much exposed raw aluminum or colored plastic and by bogus historical detail.

As a general rule, it is safe to assume that nothing is going to *look* better than the original materials from which the house was constructed and these should not be changed unless there is a good reason. Most of the items in category one—such as brickwork in the traditional colors—have a timeless quality, being both traditional and modern at the same time, and are used in much of the best new architecture; brickwork in the "new" colors on the other hand is most frequently seen on buildings that have not quite "made it" architecturally.

BRICKWORK. Good brick walls are usually a major asset to a house, and any urge to replace them or cover them over (especially with some of the synthetic materials already described) should be strongly resisted. Often this is done with the mistaken idea that it minimizes future maintenance expenses, but, in point of fact, in terms of maintenance a brick wall is one of the best possible bargains, not requiring constant painting and far outlasting any of the synthetic cover-up materials. Furthermore, the general appearance of a brick wall—unlike many building materials—usually improves with age, developing a mellow richness that, like a sort of patina, is impossible to imitate.

The pattern in which bricks are laid is known as the *Bond*; here are three of the most commonly used ones.

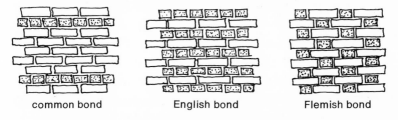

common bond   English bond   Flemish bond

The shaded bricks are called *Headers* and are laid "head-on" so that they penetrate back into the wall and help bond it together. The other bricks, laid parallel to the wall, are called *Stretchers*.

The most common maintenance tasks associated with brick walls are repointing and cleaning. Repointing consists of raking out the old mortar in all horizontal and vertical joints to a depth of about one half inch and replacing it with new—a time-consuming job usually requiring ladders and scaffolding and not generally recommended for the amateur. Furthermore, the proportion of lime to cement in the new mortar is very important in determining how porous the mix will be, and therefore how long it will last. The cost of repointing may, initially, not be much less than a cover-up job but the effect of the job can last for fifty years and more.

It should be mentioned here that if the mortar joints in an existing wall appear to have fallen out, they should be examined closely, since it is possible that the original wall was built with raked joints. In such cases the bricks were often laid to tilt slightly toward the outside of the wall, in order to drain off any water that might otherwise lie in the joints to freeze, and thus expand and break the bricks. Raked-joint walls often have rather thin joints—about an eighth of an inch wide—and if the wall is in good condition, the subtle effect of these fine, shadow-casting grooves should not be lost by stuffing them with mortar when repointing.

Cleaning brickwork can be done in two ways: by sandblasting and by washing down and scrubbing with a chemical solution such as muriatic acid. Sandblasting is a comparatively expensive process that is used when the brick is deeply stained. It tends to remove a little of the surface of the bricks and results in a clean, dry, porous, cork-like texture, so that some form of liquid sealer should be applied if the surface is exposed to the weather. A chemical wash is used for general surface cleaning and this can be done by an energetic houseowner. The scouring effect is increased by the use of a wire brush (although care must be taken not to brush out the mortar from the joints) and sometimes a broken brick, similar to the ones in the wall, makes a good abrasive rubbing tool.

Sometimes, however, the existing brickwork is of a particularly unattractive color or texture, such as some of the yellow bricks, which are not only dingy in appearance but also refuse to harmonize or contrast effectively with any known color. The owner is then faced with a problem that has only two solutions: replace the brick or cover it up. Replacing is expensive, and most of the cover-up materials look worse than the original brickwork (which at least is genuine), so painting may be the only practical alternative. This can be very attractive, particularly if the colors are kept within the "natural" range of, for instance, brick-red, terra cotta, certain warm grays and beiges, black and white —unless, of course, there is some other strong local tradition. Often the temptation just to "be different" or to run wild in color is too great, however, with unfortunate results both to the house and to the street. Therefore, unless one is equipped with an unusual ability to work with color and—even more important—with the ability to visualize *accurately* its effect on the house and the surroundings, it is best to stay within the above range.

Brickwork should only be painted if the owner is prepared to maintain it properly. It must be repainted regularly, say once every five years, the only alternative being to have it removed by chemicals or sandblasting. This fact is often not realized by those who just want a different color for the sake of change, and by the time the novelty has worn off, so has most of the paint!

One of the most common and most noticeable faults in a remodeled brick exterior are portions of new brickwork that are supposed to match the existing brick, but don't. Often great trouble has been taken to clean the old brick and match the new brick with it, but to no avail. What has been overlooked is the fact that it is also necessary for the *mortar* between the new bricks to match that between the old, with the result that the new work stands out as a series of individual bricks floating in a sea of white. The width of the mortar joint—whether it is flush with the brick or recessed—must also be matched accurately.

The whole question of the color, size, and profile of the mortar joints is of utmost importance in establishing the character of a brick wall, but for some reason is usually overlooked. Generally, the light-colored mortars should be avoided—particularly in old buildings—unless there is a strong local tradition for using them. By surrounding each brick with a strongly contrasting color one makes it into a kind of island, so that the wall becomes too "busy," appearing as a restless agglomeration of hundreds of small individual units rather than a unified surface. The darker-tinted mortars, on the other hand, emphasize the *wall* rather than the bricks, and when used with old bricks can produce textures of great richness.

One of the best ways of ensuring that the brickwork will turn out to be more or less as intended is to develop the habit of really looking at the brick walls seen every day and making a note of the ones that most nearly resemble what is wanted. The possibility and cost of reproducing them can then be discussed with a good building contractor.

CLAPBOARDING. Often referred to as siding, clapboarding is the most common form of outer face for the walls of wood frame houses and is found in most parts of the country. It takes the form of horizontal wood strips that overlap one another to keep out wind and rain, the overlaps casting continuous fine lines of shadow about four inches apart. The unique blend of sharpness and softness in these shadow lines is one of the characteristics of the wood clapboard that has not yet been successfully reproduced in other materials; in other words, nothing is likely to *look* better on a house than the original clapboards. Two of the synthetic imitations, however, although not representing any esthetic advance over their ancestors, must be mentioned for certain maintenance reasons; they are aluminum and vinyl.

Wooden clapboards do require regular painting to keep up their appearance, and if this is not done the result can look quite sad. (Also, they have been known in certain situations to shed paint in flakes after a relatively short time, although this can usually be cured by installing special vents.) The synthetic sidings, on the other hand, are relatively maintenance free, and the better-quality products come reasonably close to resembling wood—if some attention is paid to detail. They are definitely not recommended for those wishing to preserve as far as possible the original appearance of their houses, but for those who put more store in relative freedom from maintenance they are a possible choice, provided that the following points are remembered:

1. Vinyl and aluminum siding are imitation materials and to be successful must look and behave exactly like the material they are imitating. For this reason such additional effects as artificial "wood-graining," which does not appear on good wood clapboards, should be avoided.

2. Synthetic clapboards should not suddenly change their direction from horizontal to vertical when, for instance, a curved surface is encountered, just because they don't bend as easily as wood.

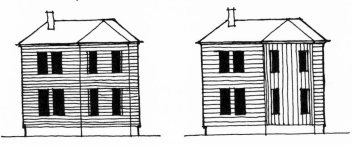

In the second illustration the vertical lines of the siding in the curved bay seem to isolate it from the rest of the building like a tower—which it is not. Also, there seems to be more than a hint of rocketry in its strong vertical thrust.

3. The spacing between the horizontal lines of the clapboards should be as near as possible to that of the original.

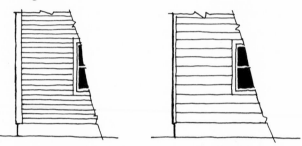

When this is widened—as is common in many of the new synthetic sidings—the scale (or apparent size) of the whole house is subtly changed, and the appearance suffers accordingly.

4. The type of treatment in which the clapboards are seen to turn the corner of a house is not a true imitation of wood and should be avoided. The original corner boards must be reproduced in wood or in the synthetic material of the clapboards *in their full original width,* since the narrow two-inch trim often used in their place just doesn't do the job visually.

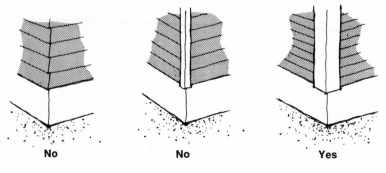

No   No   Yes

The question of the width of the corner boards is crucial when using synthetic clapboards—particularly when the original ones were particularly wide as in the case of Greek Revival houses, where they often formed pilasters or flat columns, the removal of which completely spoils the character of the house.

5. The existing trim around windows and doors should be preserved where possible or replaced by something similar.

Thousands of good old houses have lost their character by lack of attention to such simple points, the bland result having somewhat the same relationship to the original house as that of a store-window dummy to a live human being.

Vinyl siding tends to be more expensive than aluminum, but it has the added advantage of being resistant to denting; furthermore, the color is usually an integral part of the material, instead of just a surface finish, so that it cannot be removed by scratching and chipping. Aluminum siding must be electrically grounded (to minimize possible storm damage) and have some sound insulation behind it to deaden possible noise caused by driving rain or hail. Both with vinyl and aluminum, it is important that the space behind the siding be properly ventilated, since these materials, unlike wood, do not "breathe" and tend to keep moisture *in* as effectively as they keep it out.

Again, as with brickwork, one should seek out actual examples of the various materials in use before making a choice.

OTHER TYPES OF SIDING. As mentioned previously, the types of siding that claim to imitate brick and stone should be avoided. Despite much ingenuity in the copying of realistic effects of texture and color, they generally do not succeed in looking like anything other than a cheap amusement-park type imitation of the real thing. The random pattern that looks so convincing in the sample is found to repeat itself every four feet on the wall, for example, and when a corner has to be turned, the supposed "brick" or "stone" usually shows itself—its one resemblance to beauty—to be only skin deep.

In the use of materials, as in living, honesty can be said to be the best policy—and most particularly when one cannot even lie with conviction!

Asphalt and asbestos shingles, though honest in that they do not pretend to be other than they are, should also be avoided as replacements or outer covering for clapboards. When applied to walls they change the whole character of a house, usually not for the better. The fine horizontal lines of the original clapboards, which contrast so effectively with the general verticality of most old houses, are replaced by an over-all texture of small repetitive units having no particular directional bias, with the result that windows and doors, which were subtly tied in by the horizontal lines, now appear to float in a rather choppy sea.

Even when the shingles have pronounced horizontal lines, the general effect is coarser and the subtlety of the original effect is lost.

The above remarks may also apply to wood shingles when they are used as a replacement for clapboards. In their own right, however, wood shingles can be a perfectly legitimate, durable, and attractive finishing material, being generally appropriate in more rural contexts and *on houses that were originally designed for them.*

It should be mentioned that when installing any form of siding on top of the existing wall surface it is usually necessary to remove the trim around windows and doors, and either to replace it or block it out so that it relates to the new surface. This can be an important part of the cost of installation.

Before closing this section a few words must be said about the use of different materials and textures on different stories or parts of a house. This technique was used effectively on many wooden nineteenth-century houses— particularly those in the so-called Queen Anne style,* where rich and elaborate effects were often produced by a juxtaposition of textures that often included the use of both horizontal and vertical boarding on the same wall. Now, however, such contrasts in the direction of the siding or between different materials (such as clapboard and brick)

* See page 49.

tend to be used over larger areas such as whole stories, with the effect not so much of enriching the façade as of breaking it down into smaller units. Figure 1 below shows a typical example of this as applied to a rehabilitated house.

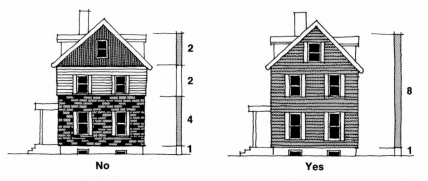

No   Yes

As shown, the end wall has been divided into four different areas of contrasting material or texture, three of which are about the same size, producing an effect rather like a layer cake. A different treatment of the same wall is shown in Figure 2: this time it is divided into only two areas, which are effectively contrasted in both size and material. The end result is simpler, more restful, and—incidentally—probably less expensive.

It will be noted that proportion comes into the picture here again—this time between the areas covered by the different materials—and that the simple ratio of 1:7 (reading upwards) in Figure 2 is much more visually effective than the rather mixed up 1:3:2:2 ratio of Figure 1.

If it is felt that the use of contrasting wall surfaces between the floors of a house is justified, the position of the "tide line," or where they meet, is of the greatest importance. Generally speaking, what goes on outside a building should have some relationship to what goes on inside, and so the tide line would be expected to express a floor or a ceiling—the only big continuous horizontal interior divisions. It is not important of course that the tide line be at *exactly* the same height as a floor or a ceiling (which are usually invisible from the outside anyway) but it is important that it should *look* as if it could be. The two treatments shown below of the same elevation illustrate this point.

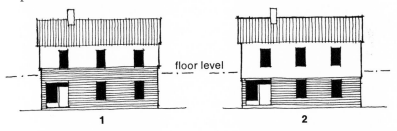

floor level

1   2

The first figure shows a commonly seen treatment, with the tide line up under the window sills of the upper floor, expressing nothing of the interior and producing a rather unstable effect through ineffective contrast of proportions. In Figure 2 the tide line has been lowered until it is actually slightly beneath the ceiling of the lower floor, in order to get more effective proportional contrast between the heights of the stories and the roof, but it looks as if the ceiling *could* be there and is therefore more logical. Also, the top story now sits more comfortably on the (apparently) smaller lower story, giving a much greater feeling of visual stability. Again, the vital statistics of 2:3:2 in Figure 2 are more effective than the 3:2:2 of Figure 1.

In both the above figures the tide line has the effect of emphasizing *horizontality*, which is not always appropriate when remodeling nineteenth-century houses, since many of them are predominantly vertical in character. Careful thought should be given, therefore, before using contrasting materials over large areas such as whole stories, if these were not in the original design. It could almost be said that only a really badly designed house would justify such a radical change.

The Use of Color

The choice of color can be a difficult—even a dangerous—subject to discuss, being of all design questions the one that is most directly influenced by personal taste. It can become, at the drop of a hat, a highly emotional issue involving the rights of the individual against those of the neighborhood or the city. Indeed, in many situations, such as the modern speculative development of almost identical and somewhat characterless houses, the individual may feel with some justification that it is only by some unique use of color that he can identify or express himself in any way. It will be assumed here, however, that the old house will have enough character to make it unnecessary to have to paint it pink and orange in order to find the way home!

The problem again is partly one of architectural good manners: how to express individuality while at the same time fitting harmoniously into the neighborhood. This need not be as sober as it sounds, however, since architectural good manners—like social good manners—can be quite flexible and do not discourage smiles and even an occasional laugh; only the equivalent of shouting or obscenities is unwelcome. Even relatively bright colors can be used with good effect at important points such as front doors without necessarily giving offense, and, in fact, they often help liven up a dull street.

There are no inflexible rules for the use of color, local traditions and climate both playing a large part in influencing people's ideas of what is right in a particular situation. What looks fine in New Orleans, for instance, may look quite out of place in Seattle or Boston and so on. Certain principles do hold good in most locations, however, and these can be translated into working suggestions—although it should be clearly stated that these suggestions are based on a current, rather than a nineteenth-century, view of the use of color in architecture and that by following them the end results may be quite different from the original color scheme of the house. The original colors of most houses are usually difficult to ascertain and, since the written accounts of nineteenth-century buildings contain few references to color, those who wish to follow a path of historical accuracy may in the end have to use their imagination almost as much as those who are designing their own color scheme. Certain colors, of course, such as cream, dark green, brown, and other earth colors are known to have been much favored in the later nineteenth century, and it may well be that some of these were the original colors of the house being rehabilitated; the author, however, must admit to being somewhat less than enthusiastic about the use of cream in general as an architectural color, and the use of brown, green, and other naturally darker colors (except black) immediately adjacent to the glass in windows, which often produces a rather dingy effect.

With these reservations in mind, which may not be shared by all readers, here, then, are the working suggestions:

1. *Do not have too many colors.*

In architecture, large areas of color are most effective when seen alone or against a background of white, black, gray, or a muted color. Two strong colors may be company

73

but three is almost certainly a crowd; therefore, paradoxically enough, in order to get the maximum effect from color one must be sparing in its use.

It should be remembered that when a roof is visible, the tiles, slates, or shingles will be part of the color scheme and must relate to the rest of the house. Therefore strong or bright colors should be avoided there if they are to be used elsewhere effectively. The traditional dark gray of slates or burnt red of tiles are still generally the best and most useful colors—whether the original material or a modern substitute is being used—because they tend to "go" with most other colors and with the environment. A tile-red roof, of course, produces a large area of color, and the rest of the house—particularly the walls—must be carefully related to it and perhaps keyed down accordingly. Slate-gray, on the other hand, will relate to (almost) anything and offers the widest possible latitude in the choice of colors elsewhere. The darker grays tend to look best on most roofs, but their use is often discouraged by asphalt-shingle salesmen on the grounds that they are reputed to draw more heat from the sun in summertime than the lighter shades. No statistics seem to be available to support this theory, however, and the author himself can report having switched over to a dark from a light gray with no noticeable difference inside a non-airconditioned house when the temperature outside was in the high nineties. There might be a small difference, which could be said to be compensated for by the amount of heat gained in the cooler seasons—both by the absorption of sunlight and by the *non*radiation of heat from inside the house. In deserts and in very hot climates, of course, these remarks will not apply; there, most likely, lighter-toned roofs will be traditional.

74

If, as previously discussed, the different stories of a house are of different materials and colors, the roof should almost certainly be gray if the over-all effect is not to be spoiled by the use of too many colors.

2. *Be careful in selecting the basic colors.*

When painting the walls of a house—whether they are made of wood or brick—one should give serious thought to the dominant color, how it will relate to colors on the other parts of the house, such as roof, doors, and windows, and also how it will relate to the street or neighborhood.

Most people (including many architects) have difficulty visualizing the precise effect of a chosen color scheme on a real building, and the finished result—for better or for worse—often comes as quite a surprise. Somehow the colors on the little samples chosen look quite different when applied to full-size walls, roofs, doors, windows, fascias, and downpipes, being either brighter or duller, better or worse, but rarely exactly as envisioned. The architect, of course, can make a colored drawing on a gray background to test the effect of his colors before painting begins, but for those people with no special drawing ability and training some simpler type of visual aid will be necessary. One of the best ways to try out colors—other than using the house itself as a guinea pig—is to make a simple flat study model from cardboard and wood. It may represent a simplified version of the street front of the house, on which most of the basic colors will appear, including that of the front door, but if this is too complicated, one can construct merely a simple rectangular wall or gable end with windows and a door. It is not important that the model be realistic in detail— only that the relative size and approximate shape of the main colored areas are reproduced and that the colors themselves are accurate. Sometimes it is difficult to match a color sample correctly, in which case one should buy a can of the actual paint to be used and paint the model with it. (If only a gallon can is available, console yourself with the thought that if the color is right, the rest can be used on the real house!)

The advantage of a model is that the parts such as walls, roofs, windows, doors, and porches can be made and painted separately and fitted together after they dry. Furthermore, the effect of different combinations can be studied, such as white trim, no shutters, yellow door, and so forth. The effects of painting the gutters and downpipes black, white, or the color of the main wall, for instance, or of painting corner posts and cornices to match the window trim instead of the main wall can also be compared simply by sticking strips of white and black paper over painted areas. Two different combinations of colors on a typical color model might appear as follows.

**Different Color Combinations on
a Simple Color Model.**

To reproduce the effect of clapboards, there are on the market several different textures of basswood obtainable at most model or hobby shops—but when using these make sure that the spacing of the lines is to the same scale as the model.

Generally speaking, a good scale for color models is one half inch on the model equaling one foot on the actual house—but it need not be calculated precisely.

It is important in all color study models, however, that the glazed part of a window be represented by *black*—this being the effect in most light conditions when seen from outside; furthermore, black, not being actually a color, will not interfere with the color balance of the rest of the model. If the window and trim are to be white—which is usually a good choice, for reasons to be discussed presently—the whole unit can be made by sticking rectangles of black paper onto a white card and adding pencil lines if desired for a more realistic effect.

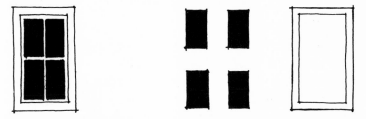

For those who may have problems in selecting a basic wall color for a wood house here are a few pointers:

White or off-white generally looks good in most situations.

Cream is usually difficult to relate to other colors, since it produces an effect of over-richness that tends to drain the life from them—especially if they are pale—and to make them seem cold; for this reason white, off-white, or very light gray-beige are preferable as trim or window colors.

Natural muted colors such as warm gray, blue-gray, beige, terra cotta, brick red, etc., go well with white or off-white trim and also usually relate well to other colors in the environment.

Pastel colors such as pale green, powder blue, violet, pink, and orange should be used mainly in very sunny climates or where there is a strong local tradition for their use. (See also page 21.)

Stronger colors such as deep brick red, barn red, dark green, etc., can look very effective with white or off-white trim, but their effect both on the house and the street should be carefully studied.

The previous remarks on the representation of glass on the color study model lead to the next suggestion:

3. *If in doubt always paint the moving parts of a window white.*

There are two good reasons for this: since the effect of the glass area from the outside is usually very dark, the window frame will contrast crisply at this most important point in the design; and a white frame and muntins will reflect light into the room instead of tending to give the effect of prison bar shadows when seen from the inside.

In many cases it will also be appropriate to paint the fixed frame of the window white (or off-white) but sometimes if it is rather wide the whole effect will be too much —especially if contrasted with a dark surrounding wall, say of brick. Here it may be useful to bring in a non-color such as black or dark gray as a kind of buffer between the white moving sash and the dark color of the wall.

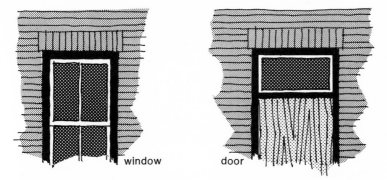

The same system should be continued at the doors, the black or dark-gray doorframe being very practical from a maintenance point of view. If there are side or top lights, the inner part of the wood frame next to the glass should be painted white (whether it moves or not) to continue the resemblance to the windows as shown above. The door will also look effective in such a frame, whether painted a bright color, left natural, or stained—which leads into the last suggestion:

4. *Keep bright colors for focal points such as the front door.*

If the original wood of the front door is in good shape, a natural or stained finish may look best, but otherwise a few coats of good paint in black, white, or a relatively strong color can be a very effective alternative. Here a semigloss paint may be desired for ease of cleaning: a high-gloss paint, however, should never be used, since it reflects too much light and distracts from the effect of the color— besides showing up every minute imperfection on the surface of the door.

The color study model can be very useful here in comparing the effect of different door colors against a selected basic house color.

VI

The Exterior: Existing Details and New Additions

It is now time to take a closer look at some of the details largely responsible for determining the character or "flavor" of a building—whether it be good, bad, or indifferent—and to examine some of the choices available at different budget levels when they are to be replaced or altered in any way. Special attention will again be given to the standard parts available on the market, so that by careful "design by selection" one may retain or improve the character of the house rather than destroy it.

The drawing on the opposite page shows a typical urban row house with the names of some of the details that formed part of the original design. Such details are found in many other types of old houses and are frequently removed, sometimes because they are damaged and are prohibitively expensive to repair or replace, but just as often because the quality of the original design is not understood or appreciated. The best features of many fine old buildings—features that were their very life—are often lost or buried forever in the process of rehabilitation and are replaced by bland, streamlined simplifications which claim to be modern and maintenance-free and which, in fact, are neither. The

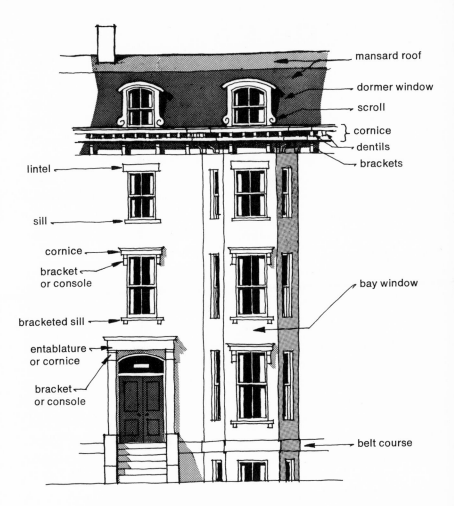

mansard roof

dormer window

scroll

} cornice

dentils

brackets

lintel

sill

cornice

bracket
or console

bracketed sill

entablature
or cornice

bracket
or console

bay window

belt course

**ROW HOUSE FRONT SHOWING SOME TYPICAL
NINETEENTH CENTURY DETAILS**

effect can be quite shocking—like meeting an old friend who has suddenly lost his hair and eyebrows.

The drawings on the opposite page show a typical nineteenth-century wooden house and what can be done to it by misdirected rehabilitation zeal. The first sketch shows the original house with essential details such as the cornice, fascia, and corner boards, which enclose the wooden clapboard walls like a picture frame. The main features such as the projecting porch and bay windows, although perhaps a little crowded together, give life to the façade by introducing light and shadow, and speak of interior space and comfort. These, plus the semi-circular-headed dormer windows, are all successfully united as one lively façade by the substantial "lid" formed by the mansard roof.

In the second sketch all the details that gave interest and the "human touch" to the original façade have been removed and the end result is a sterile and cheerless assembly of some of the worst clichés of pseudo-modernism. The thin metal gravel stop (which barely expresses the idea of a roof) is no longer an adequate lid—even for the flat and lifeless face beneath it—and does not "stop" the building properly: one feels that perhaps another story should have been added on but somehow wasn't. The entrance also is demeaned by the removal of the columned porch, which should at least have been replaced by a simplified structure of similar proportions, and the rather pathetic attempt to be "modern" by using an off-center door (in a symmetrical situation!) produces the effect of further indecisiveness. The removal of the bay window and the use of horizontally-paned "step ladder" sashes—probably in untreated aluminum—completes the job of dehumanization.

The third sketch illustrates the opposite extreme, which

No

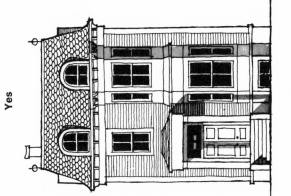

Phony Colonial or "Instant Tradition"

No

Phony Modern or "Modernistic"

Yes

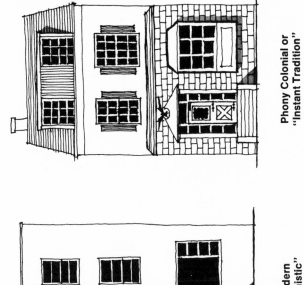

The Original Front as Designed

tries to make the house look older than it ever was by the use of bogus "historical" manufactured parts. Everything that was real in the original façade has now been replaced by a fairytale substitute: the windows have little Colonial panes, all of different sizes and proportions (the bay window is straight from Ye Olde Bargain Shoppe!) and the entrance is capped by a flat plywood imitation of a Colonial pediment complete with eagle, but without the proper cornice beneath it. The door, of course, is of the "Hans Christian Andersen" persuasion, as already described, with hinges that obviously don't work—like the undersized shutters on the windows. Finally, the change of material on the lower floor breaks up the one unifying element left—the wall.

If the pseudo-modern treatment produced a box with holes in it, the bogus historical treatment has certainly produced a doll's house.

These are, admittedly, extreme examples, incorporating as many of the typical details of each approach as is possible to show in any one façade—but how many rehabilitated buildings does one see every day on which some of these crimes have not been committed?

The case where detail has to be removed because of the impossibility of restoring or repairing it is, of course, another matter, and, if proper care is taken, the end result need not be incompatible with the principles of good design. Often the necessity for removing some part of the detail (such as the dentils of a cornice) is taken as a green light to go ahead and remove everything else, but if a policy of selective removal is followed it may be possible to preserve—perhaps even to enhance—the character of the original building. This course of action requires design skill, however, and the ability to recognize when things have gone too far.

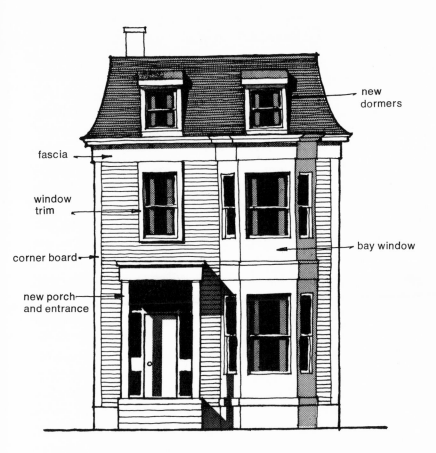

new
dormers

fascia

window
trim

corner board

new porch
and entrance

bay window

Above is the same house again—this time in a some-what simplified version. It is assumed here that most of the original detail was unsavable and had to be replaced by items readily obtainable at moderate cost. In place of the cornice there is now a fascia board deep enough to give the proper emphasis at the junction of wall and roof, and likewise the new corner boards are wide enough to make a strong visual edge to stop the horizontal lines of the clapboard. The shape, and some of the visual weight, of the original porch has also been retained in the new one—albeit in a somewhat simpler form—and the doorway itself, although of unabashedly modern design, does pick up the verticality of the original and adds a semi-circular motif of its own to offset the general effect of rectangularity. Although it has been impossible to replace the original slates on the vertical part of the mansard roof, the new dark-gray asphalt tiles are a good second choice and the general shape and visual "weight" of the original roof remains. This example also shows that even the absence of the original round-headed dormers need not be an inconsolable loss—although it is always to be hoped that some way can be found to repair rather than replace them. The width of the original window trim has been kept (as can be seen by looking at the window above the entrance, which is similar to the ones on the side and rear walls) and the shape of the bay window has not been tampered with. Finally, the new "one-over-one" windows are quite in keeping with the simple treatment of the rest of the exterior and are, incidentally, of late nineteenth-century origin anyway.

Again, this sketch is rather overloaded in an attempt to illustrate as many details as possible, but it can be said to represent generally the outer limits of what can be done to an old house—if really necessary—before its character begins to be changed radically. It stands, as it were, on the edge of uncharted territory. A skilled architect, of course, may venture even further to produce an exciting design that successfully unites the old and the new, but such experimentation is emphatically *not* for the amateur (and perhaps not even for some professionals).

It will be seen from the foregoing sketches that many of the most important details concern the windows and doorways; therefore, these two features of a house, which seem to express its character most directly and which are thus most sensitive to design changes, will be discussed in some detail.

Windows

The connection between the window and the human eye has long been recognized: the eye has been referred to as "the window of the soul," and in fact the word "window" itself is derived originally from wind-eye (which it of course was before the introduction of glass). It is not surprising then that the windows establish the basic character of many buildings in much the same way as the eyes do in a human face. Again, it is not only the eye itself—or the glass of the window—that gives the expression, but also *that which surrounds it* in the form of under-shadows, eyelashes, eyelids, and eyebrows—or, in architectural terms, sills, lintels, trim, and hood moldings. The greatest care must be taken, therefore, when replacing or remodeling these items, since the basic character of the house is being affected. Decisions such as whether or not to use shutters can be as important as choosing a pair of glasses to suit the eyes and face of a person.

However, the window itself should come first. There are so many varieties of sash on the market that it might be helpful to begin by sorting out those that are, and those that are not, useful when rehabilitating old houses. On the following page there is a typical selection of domestic sash types, which have been sorted into three broad categories: those that can almost always be used, those that should never be used, and—a most important category—those that can be used in certain situations.

In the first category are the familiar "one-over-one" and

Yes

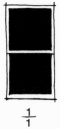 

$\frac{1}{1}$ $\frac{2}{2}$

No

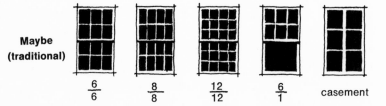

Maybe (traditional)

$\frac{6}{6}$ $\frac{8}{8}$ $\frac{12}{12}$ $\frac{6}{1}$ casement

Maybe (modern)

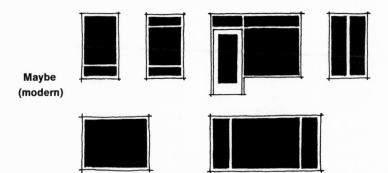

"two-over-two," referring, of course, to the number of sub-divisions in each moving sash. These styles are generally appropriate for use in houses built during the latter part of the nineteenth century, and, in addition to being histori-cally "correct," they are eminently practical, since they are easy to clean and see out of. Both of them, and some of the other styles to be discussed, belong to the mechanical category of the "double-hung" window, because each of the sashes (which move vertically) is attached to counter weights balancing the weight of the sash and so make it possible to open the window to different positions. In many of the newer versions the cord and weight combination has been replaced by a smaller and more sophisticated spring or spiral mechanism, but the principle remains the same. Be-cause of its unique weather-stopping qualities the double-hung window is widely used in most parts of the country, its principal traditional rival, the casement window (see at right in third category) being more often seen in the hotter climates, where the ability to open the entire glass area is of more immediate concern than, say, drafts from a warped sash (or rather it *was* until the advent of air conditioning). Casement windows, with their two-hinged, outward-open-ing sashes, look very different from the double-hung window, being more strongly vertical in emphasis, and they generally should not be used unless the house was *designed for them* or there is a *strong local tradition of their use.* Furthermore, it is difficult to convert from double-hung to casement win-dows, since the tall openings required by the former mean that the casements will be long and narrow, thereby pro-viding ample opportunity for drafts to get in somewhere along the long edge, which is difficult to keep weather-tight —especially if the sashes begin to warp. (To avoid this, win-dow openings are sometimes shortened by "blocking-up," with disastrous results to the appearance of the outside of the house, as shown later.)

Therefore, because of the practical and esthetic problems involved in changing window types, to say nothing of the expense involved, the homeowner would be well advised generally to stay with the existing double-hung type of window if he has them, and to spend his money on good detailing instead.

The subdivisions of the sashes themselves, however, are another matter, and in the second category of sash types— those that should never be used—there are again double-hung windows, but this time with badly proportioned panes. The panes are the smallest subdivisions in a window and their general effect should be *vertical;* if they are horizontal or square their effect can range from restlessness to vagueness—particularly in a double-hung window—and the style is neither properly traditional nor genuinely modern. Windows with horizontal subdivisions were popular in the 1920's and 1930's as a form of revolt against the general verticality of traditional architecture and became for a time an automatic guarantee of "modernity" for even the poorest building; they were soon discarded, however, as the new architecture developed self-confidence and are now merely outdated clichés. Whatever their ultimate place in architecture, it is safe to say that *windows with repeated horizontal subdivisions have no place in the rehabilitation of older houses.* In other words, the ladder or striped effect is out whether rehab is to be along traditional or modern lines.

The last window in the "not recommended" category is a familiar hybrid, consisting of a "picture" window flanked by two Colonial windows. It tries to be traditional and modern at the same time without having any real conviction either way. The basically "modern" horizontal proportion of the total opening is, of course, rarely found in an old house; if one really wants this kind of aperture, then, it would be more appropriate to use one of the better modern sash types shown in the fourth category.

The third category consists of genuinely traditional sash types—the "six-over-six," "eight-over-eight," and "twelve-over-twelve." These are basically eighteenth-century types (although some "six-over-six" windows are seen in early nineteenth-century work) and should be used *only if the style of the house requires them.* The use of "six-over-six" windows is now regarded by many developers as an automatic guarantee of Traditional Respectability—just as the horizontal pane was thought to make a building look modern not so long ago—and, along with the other standard pieces of fake historical detail already mentioned in this chapter, has resulted in the cheap debasement of the Colonial style seen almost everywhere. It is interesting to note in this connection that small panes were used in the older styles not so much for esthetic effect as because it was impossible or infeasible to make bigger ones at the time. As technology expanded so did the size of the panes, and the "two-over-two" and "one-over-one" double-hung window, with their improved visibility and cleanability, became almost standard in the latter half of the last century. These two, therefore, with the exceptions noted, are the historically "correct" sash types for most nineteenth-century houses.

A compromise such as the "six-over-one" window, though often quite attractive on certain Queen Anne houses that were designed with it originally, is not recommended generally as a later addition. Like the Colonial–picture window the "six-over-one" represents an attempt to wed historical respectability with convenience, but at least it does it with more grace.

(Such technological breakthroughs as the clip-on grids which can be installed behind the glass in a sash to give the impression of small subdivisions, but which can be removed for cleaning purposes, should of course be beneath one's contempt if the house is to look genuinely *anything!*)

The last group of windows shown in the diagram represents some of the better-proportioned modern types that can be used—albeit with discretion—when adopting a "something-old-something-new" approach to rehab. If the house is refitted entirely with these, the effect, of course, will be one of redesign rather than restoration and the greatest care must be taken in their selection. Do it only if the existing windows are completely unsuitable, and before embarking on such a course seek, if possible, the advice of a good architect.

Sometimes, however, a large modern undivided window is desired only at one place in the house—usually the living room; in that event it can often be successfully blended (or contrasted) with traditional window types on the less formal rear or side walls of the house.

In such cases the "one-over-one" window, because of its comparatively large panes, often relates quite well with the newer types and something of a "family resemblance" is preserved.

It must be stressed again, however, that window mixing requires some design skill to be done successfully, and should *not* be attempted on the more "public" sides of the house.

All the sash types just mentioned, with the exception of the "one-over-one," have subdivisions separated by what are known as muntins, which are narrower and lighter than the main frame of the sash. Generally speaking, the narrower these are the more elegant they appear—particularly when there are many subdivisions—therefore, avoid windows with fat or heavy muntins. The following sketches show cross-sections through fat and thin muntins and how this affects the appearance of the sash.

section through muntin

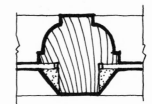

section through muntin

Right

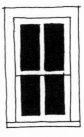

Wrong

The first is narrow and deep, allowing maximum entry of light into the room and developing its maximum strength in the out-and-in direction against external pressure from wind, etc. The second muntin is unnecessarily wide and, instead of *reflecting* light into the room, it actually *blocks* it and, from the inside, gives something of a prison-bar effect; furthermore, the extra strength developed by the width is not particularly useful, since muntins are actually prevented by the glass itself from moving in a sideways direction. Needless to say, the frames of the sashes should also not be too wide if a feeling of heaviness around the windows is to be avoided.

When selecting windows and sashes for rehabilitation work wood should always be given first preference as the material. Metal sashes tend to have a thinner and quite different appearance—unless they are imitating wood—and should be used only if modern elements are to form a deliberate part of the design. If aluminum windows are used they should have a permanent finish preferably in white, bronze, or black (with perhaps white for the moving sashes) and there should be no conspicuous areas of "natural" aluminum visible anywhere.

If one is unlucky enough to be already stuck with some exposed "natural" aluminum it can be painted with epoxy paint after treatment with a chemical etcher. This process works well on new aluminum, but where it has been exposed to the weather for some time more frequent repainting may be required, and it is well to seek advice.

Aluminum storm windows applied outside the original windows have become almost standard equipment in many parts of the country, being an efficient and easily-installed defense against cold. Unfortunately, they do not tend to enhance the appearance of an old house, and in certain cases detract from it considerably. The following suggestions are offered to those intending to use them:

1. Make sure the disposition of the sashes and the general shape of the new units reflect as closely as possible that of the inner window.
2. Avoid windows with very wide covering flanges at the edges or heavy-looking muntins between the panes.
3. Avoid "natural" aluminum finishes and select preferably a white, bronze, or black finish to match the inner window and the surrounding wood trim.

The general intention of these suggestions is to play down the new outer window and to try to make it appear as part of the house rather than an "appliance," as it often tends to seem. Success is most likely when the unit is finished in white to blend with white surrounding wood trim and inner window—irrespective of the color of the surrounding wall.

The shutter (or blind) is another of these items that, like the "six-over-six" window, supposedly confer instant respectability on any building to which they are applied. This is not to say that it is a bad or unsuitable thing in itself however, and in certain situations when properly used it can do much to enhance the general appearance of a house. The important point about shutters is not that they should work but that they should *appear* to work, and this is just what so often does not happen. The metal or plastic replicas of shutters that are now so easily obtainable on the market, even if they are reasonably convincing in themselves, are often used simply as bits of décor, with the result that they look like the wings of the kiwi bird—the vestigial remains of something once functional. The last three illustrations below show typical examples of this.

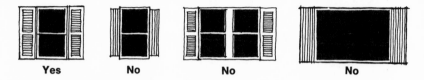

| **Yes** | **No** | **No** | **No** |

When deciding whether or not to use shutters, a basic factor to be considered is the amount of wall *between* adjacent windows; if this is less than the width of the windows themselves there will not be sufficient space for the shutters to lie flat.

| **No** | **Yes** |

If the area of wall between the windows is about the same size as the windows themselves, it will of course be completely covered by shutters and will tend to form, visually, a continuous band with the windows. The effect may or may not be attractive, depending on the character and visual "direction" of the rest of the house, and must be taken into consideration when weighing the pros and cons of shutters. Here the cardboard model, such as described in the section on the use of color, can be an invaluable tool.

While on the subject of windows, a few words must be said about the unsightly practice of "blocking up" or "blocking down" existing apertures to fit a standard window size—or perhaps to cover up a new ceiling that has been hung too low for them. This kind of visual change is most frequently seen in buildings with masonry (i.e., brick or stone) walls, where alterations to apertures can be costly, and the results tend to look like one of the following.

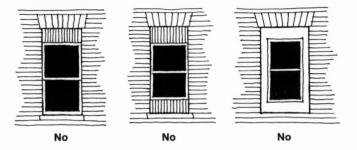

No   **No**   **No**

The temptation to do such tampering should be strongly resisted; although it may cost a little extra to get new windows the correct size for the aperture, it is money very well spent if the appearance of the house is valued.

Apertures in wood walls—although less expensive to alter—should also be generally left alone, unless, say, a window is in the wrong place or the windows in general are badly proportioned.

Entrances, Porches, and Doorways

If the windows can be considered the eyes of a building, entrances—particularly the main one—can be likened to the mouth. It is one of the main indicators of character and can appear generous or mean, symmetrical or asymmetrical, well proportioned or badly proportioned. As a result, it is often a prime target of those seeking a quick "effect" when rehabilitating, and many doors have been subjected to needless surgery when perhaps a cosmetic touch-up, in the form of a good paint job, was all that was needed. Without stretching this analogy too far it could also be said that certain raw metal additions such as "natural" aluminum storm doors have about the same eye appeal as dental braces!

(Again, the reader should be warned that there is an unusually large selection of plastic and metal door equipment, from canopies to doorknobs, all specially "designed" for the instant transformation of any doorway—but not usually for the better.)

The sketches below show three different treatments of a symmetrical entrance.

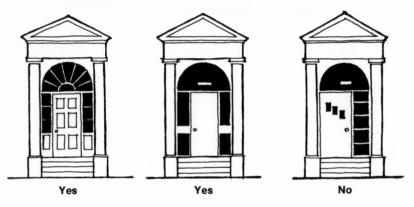

Yes　　　　　**Yes**　　　　　**No**

The figure on the left shows the original entrance, with a paneled door, sidelights, and an elegant fanlight overhead. Obviously every effort should be made to retain all of these features, but if impossible, the simplified modern treatment shown in the middle could be an attractive alternate. Note that the basic symmetry and vertical proportions of the original unit have been retained in the new design. The right-hand figure, however, is in a different category: the door has been pushed to one side and horizontal proportions introduced into the single sidelight in a mistaken effort at being "modern," with the result that the strongly symmetrical arrangement of the existing steps, porch, and fanlight is contradicted. In fact, the effect is illogical and chaotic. The "cuteness" of the diagonally stepped glass panes in the door is the last straw—but the proverbial camel's back has already been broken . . .

The door, however, does not always have to be in the center of the doorway unit, as the next sketches show.

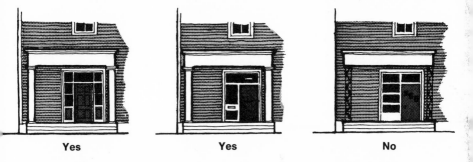

Yes   **Yes**   **No**

The original unit as shown in the left-hand figure is already in an asymmetrical situation within the framework of a broad porch. As before, every effort should be made to retain as much of the existing detail as possible but, failing this, the modern treatment shown in the middle may be a good alternative. Note that, although the original door–sidelight unit was symmetrical, the door has been set to one side in the new design—this being appropriate *when the whole unit is in an asymmetrical situation,* or when the situation is just not strongly symmetrical. In the right-hand figure, although the off-center treatment of the door is acceptable the horizontal panes in the sidelight and the stepped panes in the door are definitely not. Furthermore, the original sturdy columns have been replaced, not by simple equivalents of similar visual weight, but by feathery so-called wrought-iron supports which, though doing the job from a mechanical point of view, appear weak and inadequate under the substantial "lid" of the roof. Such accessories also happen to belong to the previously mentioned category of the "neither genuinely traditional nor honestly modern," and thus should be avoided.

If it is impossible to save the original columns of such a porch, the replacements should *appear* similar in strength, if not in detail. This warning also applies to the roof and the other parts, as illustrated at the beginning of this section in the simplified treatment of a façade. Sometimes the new columns, instead of being, say, solid six-by-sixes can be built up from standard lumber pieces or plywood as shown on the opposite page. Such columns, besides having a more interesting cross-section with some of the shadow-casting effects of a traditional molding, can provide a casing for the drainpipe from the porch roof, which is often an awkward and unsightly piece of plumbing stuck on as an afterthought. One of the sides should, of course, be made easily removable for access to the pipe in case of repair.

The visual effect of such a built-up column on the rest of the porch and on the whole front of the house must be carefully considered, however, and, if possible, studied in the form of a flat model. If it does not appear to be quite right—particularly if it seems too bulky—it should not be used.

Like the metal storm window, the metal storm door, with glazing for the winter and a screen for the summer, has become widely popular. Usually, however, because of the dissimilarity between it and the inner door, there is little chance of integrating it with the general design, and the vast majority of such doors appear simply as pieces of applied equipment. It is particularly unfortunate that this

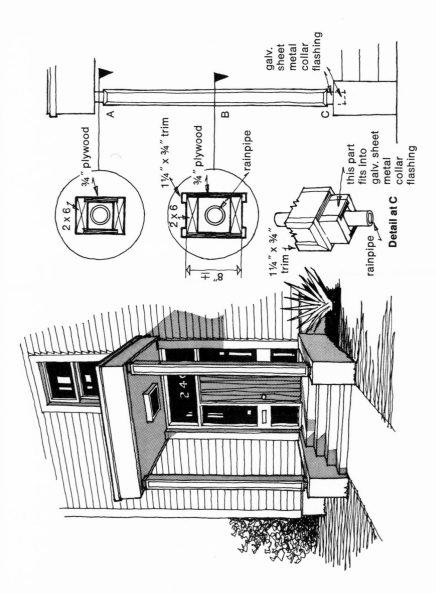

galv. sheet metal collar flashing

A

B

C

¾" plywood

2 x 6

1¼" x ¾" trim

¾" plywood

rainpipe

2 x 6

8"

this part fits into galv. sheet metal collar flashing

Detail at C

rainpipe

1¼" x ¾" trim

240

should be so at one of the key points of the design, which also has the most direct human association through physical contact.

The reason for the indigestible design quality of most outer-applied storm doors is not hard to find: if two doors are located within a few inches of each other, as is usual in this situation, they must resemble each other closely not only in general shape but also in the extent, position, and style of the glazed areas; otherwise, when both are closed, they get in each other's way visually instead of relating. The absence of such matched doors as standard items on the market and the doubtful design quality of most metal storm doors tend to put them in the category of things to be avoided. Therefore other ways of accomplishing the same end should be investigated, particularly if the original doors of the house are handsome in themselves and are part of the general design. If there is a vestibule, the problem is somewhat simplified, since the inner door (or pair of doors) can perform the function of the extra storm door or screen. Because it is located some distance from the outer door, this inner door need not resemble it so closely, although the design must be compatible and good in itself. Also, because they are set back from the face of the building, inner doors tend to belong to the interior rather than the exterior and so invite a wider variety of choice—including metal units with color finish.

If there is no possibility of having a vestibule or of matching the doors a good solution is to have only a light screen door that can be removed in the wintertime. This arrangement involves no great hardship, since most wooden entrance doors have excellent thermal insulating qualities in themselves and should need no extra protection in the winter.

Before closing this section a few words should be said about the parts of certain classical entrances which are often found in nineteenth-century houses, and which have already appeared in some of the illustrations. Figures 1 and 2 below represent two of the basic types, one with a straight entablature over the columns and the other with the entablature crowned by a triangular pediment, similar to the front of a Greek temple.

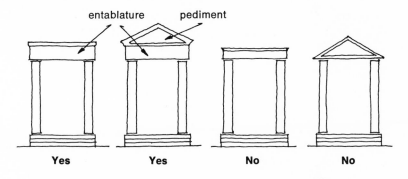

These entrances can take the form either of porches or of more-or-less flat wall decoration emphasizing the doorway (in which case the columns are referred to as pilasters). When altering or restoring such entrances it is important to see that all the essential parts are there, and in their correct proportion, or one might end up with the unsatisfactory results shown in Figures 3 and 4. In Figure 3 the entablature has been skimped, and in Figure 4 the triangular pediment sits directly on the columns without the visual "cushion" of the entablature—something that is occasionally seen in original nineteenth-century work, but which should *never* be the result of one's own efforts.

Dormers

It should be emphasized that existing dormers which are attractive or which form an important part of the original design of the house (as in the mansard or Queen Anne styles) should not generally be removed or tampered with, unless for *very* good reasons. Such reasons might be the decay of the dormer's structure or the need for headroom over a greater part of the top floor (although this would not apply in the case of a mansard). When the dormer has to be rebuilt for structural reasons the new dormer, if it cannot be an exact reproduction of the original, should at least follow along the same general lines— as in the case of the rebuilt simplified porch already described—unless, of course, the original dormers were of questionable design quality. For those intending to add *new* dormers, however, or to alter existing ones extensively, a few words of advice might be useful.

A common misconception about dormers is that, being high up in the roof, they don't need to relate to the windows in the wall underneath. While it is true that the strong visual dividing line between the materials of the roof and the wall may justify certain differences in the window treatment, there must still be a clear relationship—or family resemblance—in type or proportion. Problems of relationship most often arise when extra-wide dormers are installed to give maximum headroom over a larger area of the top story. The sketches below show, first, a traditional-size dormer with a window similar to those of the rest of the house —in width, that is, not necessarily in height. This arrangement is probably best from the point of view of appearance and the relationship between the dormer and the house as a whole: the dormer can either line up with the windows underneath (as shown in the sketch) or be located midway between them, depending on the needs of the internal plan.

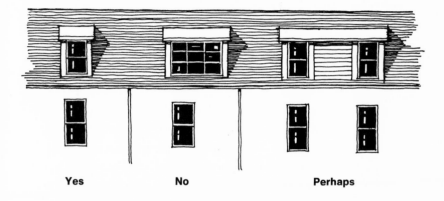

Yes   **No**   **Perhaps**

Problems of relationship begin to arise, however, with the introduction of the modern wide dormer. Figure 2 shows what often happens: some standard sash bearing no resemblance to the existing ones is introduced, and the result looks like something stuck on as an afterthought, which, of course, it really is. With a little care, an arrangement such as that shown in Figure 3 will solve both the practical and the esthetic problems, although it should be added that this would not always be recommended for use on the front of the house.

There comes a point, of course, when a dormer ceases to become a dormer. Often in the quest for extra space a whole roof is raised, as in Figure 1 below, but still obstinately insists that it is a dormer.

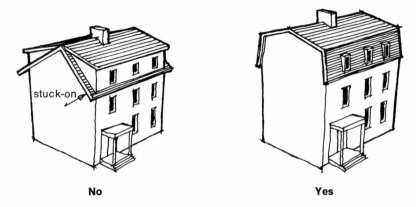

No　　　　　　　　　　　　　　**Yes**

The little snatches of "roof" at the ends and eaves are actually stuck on as pure fancy dress! In such a case, when the entire roof is being rebuilt anyway, it would be more logical to design it frankly as a mansard or a gambrel roof —as in Figure 2—a straightforward expression of a habitable roof space.

New Additions and Extensions

In the previous remarks it was mentioned that no effort need be made to imitate or fully restore dormers *of questionable design quality,* which opens up the major question of just how far it is desirable to depart from the original design of a house and its details when rehabilitating. No generalizations are possible; and each individual must decide to what extent to follow the path of historical accuracy: however, it is important that he should not limit his range of choices by falling into the habit of thinking that *everything* old is esthetically good and *everything* new esthetically bad—or that the two don't mix. (The former sentiments may be music to the ears of the antique dealer but should not survive two minutes of serious thought.)

The possibility of adding new modern elements carefully and sympathetically designed, therefore, should never be overlooked. Also, in whatever style chosen, it is often possible to actually *improve* the original design by addition.

Whether the results are considered "improvement" or just "peaceful co-existence," however, some of the ways in which new work can relate to old should be examined. These are almost identical to those listed under "Basic Ways in Which a Remodeled Exterior Can Relate Itself to the Street or Neighborhood" on page 56. Again it is not necessary to try to relate to the old part of the house in *every* way—perhaps only three or four ways may be enough.

The drawing on the following page shows some of the possible approaches to the problem of adding a new wing to the rear of an old detached house: the top sketches illustrate what might be termed the "traditional" approach, in which the style of the original building is duplicated or followed as closely as possible, and the middle sketches show ways of adding modern elements that are sympathetic to the original architecture. The bottom sketches show what *not* to do.

In Figures 1 and 2—the "traditional" approach—it will be noted that the wall face of the new extensions has been kept back a little from the wall face of the older structure. This setback not only helps articulate the new wing clearly but also avoids the flush joining of old and new materials —a feature which can be both awkward and embarrassing if the materials don't match exactly. From the design point of view, when two such walls are on different planes, there can be greater latitude in the extent to which materials and details need resemble one another; if, on the other hand, the walls are on the *same* plane, the materials and details should match closely. One of the principal

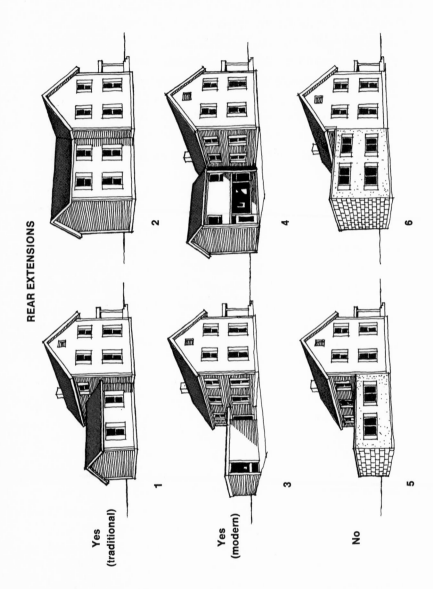

REAR EXTENSIONS

Yes
(traditional)

Yes
(modern)

No

1

2

3

4

5

6

faults of the extensions shown in Figures 5 and 6 is that although the walls of the old and the new work are flush with each other—making them in effect one single wall— the materials and details used in each section have nothing at all in common with each other.

The modern extensions shown in Figures 3 and 4, although not imitating the detail of the older part of the house, nevertheless relate to it quite well by picking up some of its basic characteristics. The materials of the walls and (in Figure 4) the roofs, for instance, are the same, and the floors of the new wing line up with those of the old, giving the same feeling of scale to both parts. Furthermore, some effort has been made in the new work to follow the vertical proportions of the window openings in the old house, so that the general directional emphasis of both sections is about the same. Note also that in both cases the new work has been carefully "buffered" from the old, so that the main walls do not make direct contact. In Figure 3 this is done by putting a recessed doorway at the point of intersection, and in Figure 4 by using a recessed link somewhat similar in effect to the link between Pullman cars.

Figures 3 and 4 show the wall of the new wing pushed well back to illustrate the possibility of creating a pleasant outdoor living space sheltered by the two sections of the house and with some larger windows and doors opening onto it—this also being possible when using more "traditional" solutions. When space is limited in such a case it may be necessary, in order to have as big a courtyard as possible, to push the new wing back until it can't go any further —in other words, until the walls of the new wing and old section are lining up in the rear. Here the "buffer" link again saves the day, however, and, although the two walls are on the same plane, they are nevertheless *separated*—producing the same effect as if they had been on a different plane.

A link quite clearly expresses the fact that an extension *is* an extension and, provided that it has been well designed and built, there need be no reason for wanting to hide the fact.

Many of the things *not* to do, shown in Figures 5 and 6, are, unfortunately, all too often done. These particular illustrations could represent, say, a concrete block addition (with metal windows) to a wooden clapboard house. No effort has been made to relate the new wing to the existing house in material, detail, proportions, or directional emphasis; on top of all this, the new wall is on the same plane as the old one. The only ray of hope left is that some conveniently located rain downpipe could be used to hide the thoroughly nasty joint between the wall surfaces.

Before closing this section, a final note should be added about the pitch, or slope, of roofs. When altering or building onto a house, one should not, generally speaking, add roofs at different pitches to that of the original. If in Figure 4 above, for instance, the extension had a low-pitched roof, much of the continuity between the old and new wings would have been lost. Sometimes a flat roof can relate to a pitched roof (as in Figure 3), but a pitched roof does not usually relate well to a roof of another pitch. The practice of using different pitches on the two sides of the *same* roof is also usually bad—especially in a rehabilitation context—because, besides being "nonhistorical," it tends to make the roof look as if it were sliding off the building.

VII

The Interior: How to Measure and Draw Existing Conditions

If one is intending to alter the interior of one's house or apartment to any extent it is essential to have some reasonably accurate drawings of the existing layout so that one knows *exactly* what there is to work with. This is often quite different from what one *imagines* one has, with the result that many rehab layouts built from only verbal instructions or sketches on the back of an envelope have serious snags, such as not enough room to have a clothes closet or, if there is one, not enough room to hang the coats properly in it, no space for a door to swing into the bathroom, and so forth. These problems and many others will be discussed in Chapter VIII.

Also, in most parts of the country, drawings showing the existing conditions with the proposed alterations must be submitted to the local government Building Department before a building permit can be obtained, to make sure that the health and safety requirements of the local building code have been met (i.e., structural soundness, adequate daylight and ventilation, and provision for emergency fire exits). If the federal government is providing any of the money to finance the work, it will also require some graphic proof that its own requirements are being met.

Whether or not it is legally necessary to have drawings (which should be checked into), it is certainly better to have something to refer to even if one is only replanning the furniture layout of a room. By spending a little time measuring and drawing up a room accurately and by moving around bits of cardboard scaled to represent the furniture, it is possible to find out just what will work and what won't and to get new ideas for groupings that otherwise might not have been considered. Much energy—and even marriages —can be saved by *not* trundling the real sofa to the other end of the room only to discover that it doesn't really fit there.

This chapter, therefore, is about *drawings*—how to read them, which is not as difficult as it may seem, and which concerns anyone thinking of signing a building contract; and how to measure and draw up a simple existing layout.

Reading a Drawing

Apart from the design drawings, which are usually produced in the initial design stage to show how the work is being laid out and how it will look when completed, the most important drawings are the working drawings. These are the drawings from which the builder will work and—most important—being part of the contract, they are also the owner's last opportunity to check the proposals before they become reality.

In trying to understand working drawings, many people are put off by the apparent complexity, the lines of the actual drawing often being difficult to read against all the dimensions and notes that are a necessary part of the information required by the builder. Nevertheless, although it cannot compete with a design drawing for illustrative clarity, a good working drawing should not be too difficult to read and should still be a *drawing* with incidental notes and not the other way around. Making the "visual" part read clearly through the "verbal" is an elementary design problem in itself (and, incidentally, may give us a clue as to the abilities of the architect or designer responsible for the work).

Working drawings consist basically of *Plans*, *Sections*, *Elevations*, and *Details*.

The *Plan*, or layout, is what one would see looking directly down if an imaginary giant rip-saw were to cut horizontally through all the walls and partitions of the house at a height of about four or five feet above the level of the particular floor being illustrated and everything above this line were to be lifted away. (The cut occurs about this height because if lower or higher it would pass below or above the window openings and they would not appear in the drawing.) All features such as walls, partitions, doors, windows, and so forth should appear on the plan and be located when necessary by appropriate dimensions. Movables such as furniture—which should be shown on every good design plan—do not appear on working drawings, since they are not part of the building contract.

Although the plan could be legitimately described as a horizontal section (or cut), the term *Section* is generally used to describe the vertical cuts made through the house by the hypothetical saw and also both the vertical *and* horizontal slices through special details such as windows and dormers, which show exactly how they are to be constructed.

The *Elevations* are the familiar drawings of the outside of the house (or of important interior walls, etc.), which show the general shape and also the location and shape of all the principal features such as roof, gutters, doors, and windows on the outside, or windows, doors, shelves, cabinets, and radiators on the inside. More than any of the other drawings they show us what things will *look* like—although in a working drawing, unlike a design drawing, it is the *location* and *dimensions* of the parts that are being illustrated rather than their appearance. The term "elevation" here means literally the "elevating," or drawing in a vertical position the walls or planes that appear only as lines on the plan, and this meaning should not be confused with the other, used in land surveying—the relative altitude of a point.

Details have already been referred to in the remarks on *Sections* above, but they may also include elevations and plans of special features, or small areas, of the building. It is from these that the particularly important parts of the work, such as windows, stairs, balconies, and porches, are constructed. Working drawings all too often skimp on such details, with results that range from the unfortunate to the disastrous. It cannot be overemphasized that if any part of the work is not entirely standard, it must be *drawn properly in detail.* If this is not done it will be "designed" on the spot by the person who has the problem of building it—to the delight or disappointment of the owner . . . Proper details may take a few extra hours of drafting time, but it's well to heed the old Scottish adage and not "spoil the boat for a ha'penny-worth of tar"!

In rehabilitation work involving mainly interior redesign the plan is usually the most important—and sometimes the only—working drawing. On the opposite page is a typical layout plan such as would be seen in the working drawings

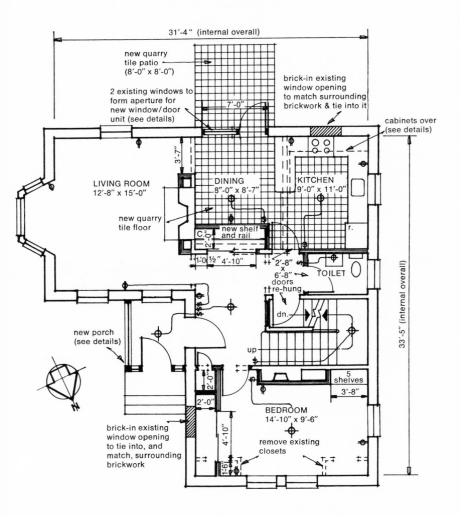

31'-4" (internal overall)

new quarry
tile patio
(8'-0" x 8'-0")

brick-in existing
window opening
to match surrounding
brickwork & tie into it

2 existing windows to
form aperture for
new window/door
unit (see details)

7'-0"

cabinets over
(see details)

3'-7"

LIVING ROOM
12'-8" x 15'-0"

DINING
8"-0" x 8'-7"

KITCHEN
9'-0" x 11'-0"

new quarry
tile floor

new shelf
and rail

r.

C

2'-0"

1'-0" ½" 4'-10"

2'-8"
x
6'-8"
doors
re-hung

TOILET

33'-5" (internal overall)

dn.

new porch
(see details)

up

5
shelves

3'-8"

2'-0"

2'-0"

brick-in existing
window opening
to tie into, and
match, surrounding
brickwork

4'-10"

BEDROOM
14'-10" x 9'-6"

remove existing
closets

1'-6"

N

FIRST FLOOR PLAN

for a small to medium-sized rehab job. Here is a list of the basic information it contains:

1. The existing walls and partitions to remain—shown unshaded.
2. The existing walls and partitions to be removed—shown in broken lines.
3. New walls and partitions—shown shaded according to a key that represents the various materials used.

wood stud   brick   concrete block

4. Enough (but not too many) dimensions to locate all new work in relation to existing walls and partitions; note that all the essential dimensions such as the 5'-0" for the bath in the bathroom, the 3'-6" corridor, etc., are clearly stated, whereas certain dimensions that may vary slightly on the job without serious consequence are followed by a "plus or minus" sign, indicating that if there is any discrepancy between the dimensions on the drawing and the actual work, the difference should be adjusted at that point.
5. All existing and new door and window openings and any changes being made to the existing ones.
6. Full *quarter-circle* door swings for all new and remaining doors; this is a useful check for certain trouble spots such as doors that are likely to hit one another frequently (or that need to have a notch cut out of one side to let them swing past the toilet in the bathroom)!

7. The position of all new fixed electrical items; here are some of the symbols most commonly used.

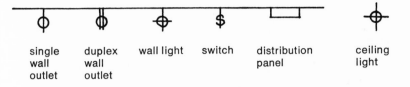

| single wall outlet | duplex wall outlet | wall light | switch | distribution panel | ceiling light |

Whenever symbols of any kind are used on a drawing there should be a key somewhere showing clearly what each symbol means. Another essential piece of information is the *scale* to which the particular sheet or item is drawn, or the relationship of the size of the drawing to the real thing (i.e., scale $\frac{1}{4}'' = 1'\text{-}0''$; or one fourth of an inch on the drawing equals one foot of the building). A North point, which is a must in any land plan, can be useful also on floor plans of houses to show clearly which are the sunny and the non-sunny rooms. Some local authorities ask for all room sizes to be shown on the plan either by dimension arrows or by a note such as "Living Room—11'-9" × 17'-6" ": this request includes both new rooms and rooms that will remain unchanged in the new layout.

The reader should use the above notes as a checklist when looking at working drawings. Not all these items will be relevant to every job, of course, and extra information will usually be needed, but they do give an idea of what the basic essentials of a working drawing are.

For those who are interested in doing some drawing themselves, the following notes have been put together as a simple guide to measuring and drawing the interior of a house or apartment (or even a room) for the purpose of replanning or refurnishing.

Measuring

The basic tools required are:

1. A 50 ft. minimum measuring tape—or a 6 to 10 ft. tape if only a room is being measured. The tape should be subdivided into *inches* and not tenths of a foot (as in the case of an engineer's tape).
2. A yardstick or rigid rule for measuring heights.
3. A pad or clipboard with sheets of paper at least 8½″ × 11″.
4. A medium-grade pencil—not too hard, not too soft —and a means of sharpening it.
5. An eraser (!).

Before using the tape, a simple outline sketch of the present layout of the floor of the house or the room to be measured must be made, somewhat like the one on the opposite page (which is of the same house as the working drawing example). If the whole floor is being measured, as here, it is worthwhile to try to approximate the proportion and relative position of the rooms as closely as possible to the real thing as can be judged by eye, thereby making the later stage of "drawing-up" that much simpler. Your first result will probably not look much like the illustration, but with practice it is possible to sketch layouts quite accurately (the author has found that certain sketches made on the job have proved not only to be proportionally accurate but to have been subconsciously drawn to a scale of ¼″ = 1′-0″!). It is not always necessary to represent partitions and walls by double lines, as in the somewhat sophisticated illustration, and often a single line diagram is quite enough—provided that any suspected deviations from the standard partition thickness (usually about five inches) are noted. If only one

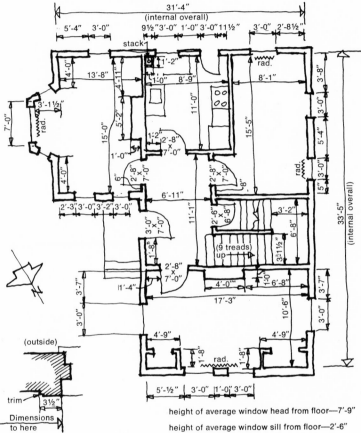

height of average window head from floor—7'-9"

height of average window sill from floor—2'-6"

height from 1st to 2nd floors—9'-10"

(outside)

trim

Dimensions to here

Typical window jamb

room is being measured, of course, one won't get involved with wall or partition thicknesses at all. But however simple the technique, the sketch *must* show all projections, recesses, windows, doors, and doorswings, and should be *as large as the sheet of paper will allow* so that there is plenty of room to put in *legible* dimensions. Although plain paper is preferable, those who may have a little trouble drawing a straight line may prefer to work on paper with lightly printed squares; these, however, should only be used as guidelines that can be departed from and not as a system of railway tracks for the pencil point!

With the rough sketch in hand and someone to hold the other end of the tape, the actual measuring can begin.

To avoid needless frustration later on, all measurements should be legible, accurate, and taken at the right places— elementary but crucial advice.

If the place being surveyed is one's own house or apartment, legibility may not be quite so important, since any unclear dimension can be checked immediately, but if it is a place as yet unoccupied, too many return visits may be inconvenient or embarrassing, so a higher performance standard will be necessary. A word of comfort may be needed here, however: it is *most* unlikely that you will get all the information required in one visit—even architects rarely do—so don't be needlessly discouraged.

Accuracy, for the purposes of a rehab survey, need only be to the nearest half inch—that is, an actual measurement of 8'-7¼" would be put down as 8'-7", 8'-7⅝" as 8'-7½", and so forth. Only in exceptional cases is it necessary to use smaller fractions of an inch.

To make sure that the measurements are taken at the right place and that time is not wasted in needless duplication, the following checklist has been prepared, giving the essential steps in working sequence (those measuring only a room will, of course, begin with the second step). Special attention should be paid to such items as the heights of ceilings and windows, which are all too often overlooked at the time of measuring. Finally, it should be pointed out that *all measurements should be taken to the plaster or wall surface* and not to baseboards or projecting wooden trim.

Checklist of dimensions and information required in making a measured drawing

1. The first dimensions taken should always be the over-all internal sizes of the house or apartment (or floor of the house or apartment) one is intending to measure. If the measurements are not done right away, it is a safe bet that they will be forgotten about later and, as a result, the final drawing may be quite inaccurate. The over-all sizes should *never* have to be arrived at later by adding up a string of room sizes and partition thicknesses but, on the contrary, should act as a check to these smaller sizes. Often, wall or partition thicknesses that are difficult to measure can be found by subtracting from an over-all dimension all the room or space sizes that lie along its path, the result being the combined thicknesses of all the walls and partitions that cross its path; from this figure the thickness of the individual partitions can be arrived at quite easily. In the survey sketch example on page 119 if one subtracts from the over-all size of 31'-4" the combined sizes of the rooms and spaces included (i.e., 13'-8" + 8'-9" + 8'-1" = 30'-6"), one finds that the combined thicknesses of the two partitions included is 10", which makes them each 5" thick—about average for a wood stud partition. If

the combined thicknesses of the partitions seem to work out in excess of an average of five to six inches per partition, one of them is probably a fattened pipe space, or chase, the actual position of which must be checked and shown on the drawing.

2. The next step is measuring the rooms themselves, and again the over-all sizes must be taken *first* before going on to measure the position of the projections, alcoves, windows, and doors. *The "inchworm" method of crawling around the perimeter of a room measuring everything that pops in or out is not enough in itself without the over-all sizes as checks.*

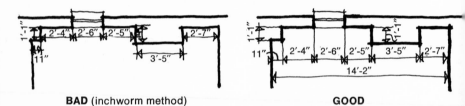

BAD (inchworm method)   **GOOD**

3. If there is any cause to suspect that the building or room being measured is not quite square, a few diagonal measurements should be taken in addition to the other room sizes so that the true shape of the room can be drawn. It does no harm to take a few

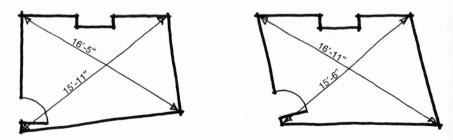

diagonal measurements anyway, in case there is a serious distortion that isn't obvious.

Irregular rooms and buildings are much more common than most people suspect, particularly in dense urban areas, and in fact many of the greatest architectural masterpieces, such as Sir Christopher Wren's London churches, conform to highly irregular sites. There is usually nothing to get worried about, therefore, if this happens to be the case, as long as the irregularities appear in the drawing, and the furniture, doorswings, and so forth are planned with these in mind.

4. When measuring within the rooms make sure you take only useful sizes and no more than necessary to locate all the major features already mentioned. All one usually needs to know about a door, for instance, can be summed up by noting its size and its distance from the nearest wall.

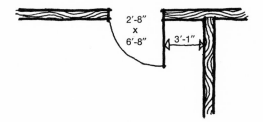

5. In addition to locating windows and doors accurately, it is wise to make a sketch of a section (or profile) through the side of a typical door or window opening showing its general shape and where the dimensions were taken to. This is called the jamb section and is particularly important if one is intending to build new partitions alongside it, as seen in Chapter X. The

new partitions must relate properly to the trim, the woodwork around windows or doors, and not just slap into it any old way, as so often done in the more "improvised" type of rehabilitation.

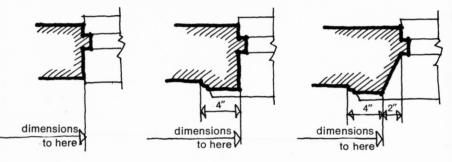

6. Don't forget to make a note of any heights that may affect what can or cannot be done in remodeling; these might include the floor-to-ceiling height, the floor-to-floor height, the height of window sills and heads from the floor, and the height of doors (as already mentioned). The amount of clearance under a stairway, duct, or sloping ceiling may also be important in determining how a layout should be shaped.

7. Existing stairways should be carefully sketched and, in addition to the over-all size and width of the runs, a note should be made of the number of treads and risers from floor to floor and also whether there are winders or not.

8. Finally, check that all elements which might be difficult or expensive to remove, such as flues or chimney breasts, stacks, and pipes, have been properly located and noted on the sketch. Structural walls should be noted and not confused with the extra-

thick partitions used for pipe spaces or pocket sliding doors. (In the next chapter is described a way to easily locate structural walls.)

You should now be ready to draw up your house or room from the measured survey—always allowing for the fact that, if you don't live in it, you will almost certainly have to return at *least* once to check suspicious dimensions, to find out how high the window sills really are where you propose to have a new kitchen, or to find out finally just which walls and partitions are holding up the house!

Drawing Up from the Measurements

If one is just drawing up a room for a furnishing plan the only tools required are a pencil, a straightedge of some sort, and a sheet of squared paper; the squares should be preferably one fourth of an inch, so that each one will represent one foot of the real room at a scale of $\frac{1}{4}'' = 1'\text{-}0''$. The procedure is straightforward and needs no description.

For drawing up a whole house or floor, however, or if one wants to graduate from the rather unsophisticated squared-paper technique, a few extra tools are needed: a small drawing board, a T square or parallel rule, a triangle, a pair of compasses or a circle template, and an architect's scale. An engineer's scale should not be used because the feet are subdivided into *tenths* instead of *twelfths* of inches, which are more generally used and are standard in the building world; remember that however strongly one may feel about the superiority of the decimal system, the builder's rule is *not* divided into tenths of a foot and he will be understandably reluctant to perform feats of mathematics in order to build the job.

The basic tools are illustrated on the opposite page. The drawing board need not be larger than about 30″ × 24″ for the average drawing of a floor of a house and in many cases a smaller one will suffice; likewise, the basic T square and triangle are all that is needed for the best work. The parallel rule and adjustable triangle shown in the second illustration are standard tools of the architect, but they are a little more expensive and are not really necessary unless they are going to be used often. Also, a cheap pair of school compasses— the kind that holds the stub of a pencil—will draw door swings as well as on the best architectural models (the author has to confess that his most reliable pair of compasses was purchased in his early youth from a well-known international "five and ten" and has outlasted most of his more pretentious circle-making equipment).

Armed, then, with these simple and relatively inexpensive instruments, you have all that is necessary to produce the best drawings—the rest is up to you.

Using a pencil that is a little harder than the one used for the survey (say an H or 2H), you can proceed to draw up the plan from the measured sketch and notes. A medium grade of tracing paper—neither too rough nor too greasy— should be used and held down to the board on all four corners by small tabs of masking tape. (If you can buy the tracing paper by the sheet it will be more economical than buying it by the roll—unless you intend to use large quantities of it.) Basically, the T square will enable you to draw all the parallel horizontal lines on the sheet, and the triangle to draw all the vertical lines at right angles to these. From here on the checklist of information to be included in a working drawing and the example of a working drawing already given earlier in this chapter will be useful as a general guide—especially if you mean to include proposed changes

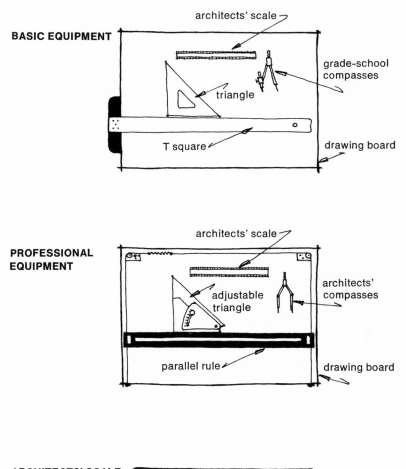

BASIC EQUIPMENT

architects' scale

grade-school compasses

triangle

T square

drawing board

PROFESSIONAL EQUIPMENT

architects' scale

adjustable triangle

architects' compasses

parallel rule

drawing board

ARCHITECTS' SCALE

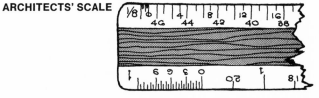

as well as existing conditions. Whether producing workable working drawings or just recording the existing building, however, it is essential that the drawings be clearly readable; to this end, all things shown in *section* (i.e., cut open by the imaginary rip-saw) should be outlined by a line that is both darker and a little fatter than the other lines on the sheet. This is a simple point, but it is often overlooked— even by some professional draftsmen—with the result that simple drawings appear needlessly complicated and about as legible as the traditional doctor's handwriting.

There are many elements in drafting that can only be learned from experience, but by referring to these diagrams and notes and going as far as he feels his ability will take him, the average reader should find it possible to produce accurate and useful drawings of whatever he intends to re-habilitate. Even if the drawings are not finally used as working drawings, the experience of having drawn them up may save some time and labor on someone else's part and will certainly put the houseowner in a better position to understand, and perhaps to solve, many of his remodeling problems.

VIII

The Interior: Planning the General Layout

Many existing houses and apartments do not work properly—or not as well as they might—because the rooms are badly located or are the wrong shape and size for their purpose. Furthermore, many rooms give the impression that the designer—if indeed there ever was one—gave no thought to the possible location of furniture within them. This last fault, in fact, is so common in older houses that the following chapter will be devoted to the rooms themselves and how to design *with* furniture. Before this, however, it is necessary to discuss *where* the rooms should go ideally and how one might go about improving the layout of the house whether one intends to start from scratch or merely to shift a partition or block up a door. Perhaps even those who have no thought of remodeling may get some ideas for some small and relatively inexpensive changes that might permit a new and better use of the existing rooms.

At the very least, the reader of this chapter will be in a better position to judge how well his existing layout works.

The General Layout

When designing (or making design decisions) for remodeling, the interests of three different parties must be considered: the owner (or user), the law, and the building contractor. Basically, the owner wants the job to be efficient and attractive, the law wants it safe and hygienic, and the builder wants it to be reasonably easy to construct. Actually, all these requirements turn out to be in the best interests of the owner, as he would not wish to live in a firetrap with unsanitary drains, nor pay the bills for unnecessarily expensive construction. Of all these requirements, those of the law are the most specific, and therefore any compromises to be made will tend to affect the efficiency, appearance, and cost of the building rather than the safety of its inhabitants. A good design will strike the right balance between these variables, getting maximum workability and appearance for a given construction cost.

At no time do the requirements of the owner, law, and builder, however, seem to be most at odds than when planning an interior layout from scratch.

For instance, if one is remodeling a row house that has windows only on the front and rear walls, there may be a dilemma as to where to place the kitchen. If it is against the outside wall, it will have natural daylight and ventilation—an arrangement pleasing to whomever cooks—but then a lot of spare space in the interior will be left, usable only for rooms and areas that do not absolutely require direct daylight, i.e., bathrooms, eating areas, or storage closets. As there is a limit to the useful amount of such accommodation, the result may be a rather inefficient layout with an embarrassment of under-used space in the middle— see Figure 1 in the opposite diagram. On the other hand, by putting the kitchen deep in the interior, an extra bedroom is gained and there is a better proportional relationship between all the rooms. The law has its say in all this by insisting, quite reasonably, that all living rooms and

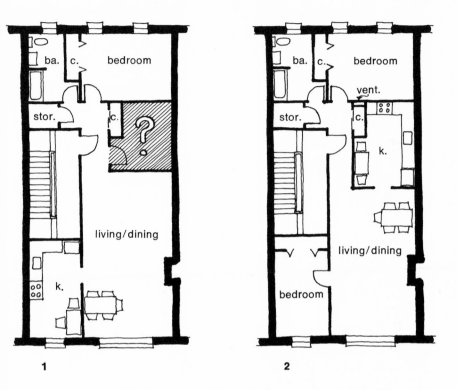

1   2

bedrooms shall have natural light and ventilation and that
kitchens and bathrooms should have ventilation—natural or
mechanical. Therefore, in the second layout the price of
extra mechanical ventilation for the kitchen must be added
—which brings in the cost factor.

Which of these plans is adopted may depend on the
amount of time spent in the kitchen during daylight hours,
or, perhaps more important, on the number of bedrooms
required for the family.

Proportion is mentioned here again—this time in connection with the relative sizes of rooms. This can be very

important, and one of the first things one should do when judging a layout is to check quickly if the living room is larger than the bedrooms; if it is not, that fact clearly indicates that space is not being used to the best advantage.

The rooms and spaces in a house or apartment can be broken down into four main categories—*living, utility, storage,* and *circulation.* Living rooms and bedrooms come under the heading of living and should generally have daylight, the better views, and the lion's share of the space. The utility section includes kitchens, bathrooms, and utility rooms, and these may or may not have daylight and views, according to the number of windows that are available or the wishes of the owner. It is, of course, desirable that both kitchens and bathrooms should have daylight and natural ventilation, but this is not always possible, as already seen—particularly in urban areas. Sometimes only one such room can have a window, and if so it is usually preferable for it to be in the kitchen, where more time tends to be spent. Where it is impossible for either or both to have a window, mechanical ventilation is acceptable in most local building codes (indeed, so precious has outer wall space with windows become that in nearly all new apartment blocks, the kitchens and bathrooms are located in the center of the building in a "service core," making it possible to design deeper apartments and to avoid the long, thin slab of a building that uses up so much land).

Of storage and circulation, more will be said later on; here, it need only be mentioned that storage must be conveniently located, and circulation, i.e., corridors and stairs, should be kept to a minimum.

An excellent guide to the relative areas required for the various rooms and spaces can be found in the *Rehabilita-*

tion Guide for Residential Properties (HUD's manual PG-50), published by the U.S. Department of Housing and Urban Development. The table of recommended minimum sizes for rooms is reproduced on the following pages, but the Building Planning Section of HUD's manual PG-50 (see Appendix B) contains so much useful information that it is well worth reading. If a federal loan is being used to finance the job, of course, these standards are mandatory, but otherwise they can be very useful to give the homeowner a good idea of what should be expected of a good layout or what may be required by the local building laws—always remembering that the standards suggested are *minimal* and not average.

Adherence to minimum standards, however, does not guarantee a good design of layout, and other factors must be taken into consideration when deciding which room goes where: these are *Orientation, Adjacency,* and, last but not least, *Economy.*

Orientation

First, the rooms and spaces must be "oriented" or "orientated" to the best advantage. That is, they must make the best use of available sunlight and views. Generally speaking, it is thought desirable to have the living room windows nearest the south for maximum sunlight, but this is not an inflexible rule. There may, for instance, be an outstanding—or perhaps just a more desirable—view on the other side of the house to attract the living functions in that direction and reverse the whole plan. Often in urban situations, the living room faces the street just because "it has always been there," whereas the rear yard

Table R4-1
ROOM SIZES

Name of Space(1)	Minimum Area (Sq. Ft.) (2)			Least Dimension(2)
	O-BR LU	1 & 2 BR LU	3 or more BR LU	
LR	NA	140	150	10'-0"
DR	NA	80	100	7'-8"
K	NA	50	60	5'-4"
K'ette	20	25	40	3'-6"
BR (Double)	NA	110	110	8'-8"
BR (Single)	NA	70	70	7'-0"
LR-DA	NA	180	200	(3)
LR-DA-K	NA	220	250	(3)
LR-DA-SL	220	NA	NA	(3)
LR-SL	190	NA	NA	(3)
K-DA	80	80	110	(3)
K'ette-DA	60	60	90	(3)

NOTES:

(1) Abbreviations:

LU = Living Unit   K'ette = Kitchenette
LR = Living Room   BR = Bedroom
DR = Dining Room   SL = Sleeping Area
DA = Dining Area   NA = Not Applicable
K = Kitchen   O-BR = No separate bedroom

(2) Variations to these areas and dimensions may be permitted when existing partitions preclude precise compliance, and the available area or dimensions do not hinder furniture placement and the normal use of the space.

(3) The least dimension of each room function applies, except for the overlap or double use of space in combination rooms.

GUIDES

G401-2 The floor areas given in Table R4-1 are minimum for healthy occupancy in order to reflect maximum construction economy but the combining of these minimums in planning living units is not recommended. Only plan layouts which provide successfully for closet and window location, door swings and furniture placement will determine whether minimum space will result in acceptable livability.

could be made the more attractive and private focal point for living. Often so-called picture windows are installed near the sidewalk line on a busy street, in a misguided effort to "modernize," and the occupants find out later that it is they rather than the street that become the subject of the "picture"! Heavy drapes are then installed and kept permanently drawn, canceling out the original intention and wasting money. Furthermore, the chances are that the picture window has not improved the appearance of the outside of the house, so that bad orientation becomes bad design as well as bad economy.

The factor of cost, of course, may enter into orientation decision-making. It may be that in order to get the living room in the ideal situation, certain structural walls have to be removed, which means that beams must be introduced to support the load coming down on them from upstairs. Should this prove too costly it may be necessary to settle on another location for the living room that fits more readily into the existing structural system. Also, it must be remembered that beams, if introduced, must be deep enough to take their load (the longer their span the deeper the beams), and unless they are to be covered up by a hung ceiling they are visible and thus become visual elements in the design. Few things are more distracting in a living room ceiling than a solitary beam that relates to nothing in the room layout underneath—visible evidence that the structural system and the layout are not in harmony, as in Figure 1 on the opposite page.

If properly located, however—say between the living and dining areas of a living/dining room—the beam then may become a positive design element emphasizing the different functions of the space beneath, as in Figure 2, and can

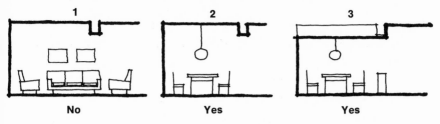

even be used as the edge of a dropped ceiling over one of the areas, as in Figure 3.

While on the subject, a few words should be said about structural walls and beams. The structural walls of a nine-teenth-century house are simply the walls that support the *ends* of the joists (or beams), which in turn support the floors and roof. If the joists pass continuously and without joints over the top of an internal partition, it is unlikely that that partition is being used as a structural wall, but if the joists *end* there and are overlapped or jointed in any way the partition is certainly a structural wall and its re-moval will cause the floor above to fall in or sag. Since it is not always possible to poke around inside floors and ceil-ings to find out all this, the best way of discovering which are the structural walls is to visit the basement or the low-est point in the house. Structural walls by their nature must transfer their loads to the ground, and they will be clearly visible in the basement as walls, partitions, or rows of col-umns. All partitions in the basement, of course, may not be structural walls and it is necessary to follow them up through the building to see if they are continuous.

Beams replacing structural walls can be of steel where maximum strength with the least depth is required, but usually they are of wood for the sake of economy, often taking the form of two or three joists laid side by side. A rough idea of proper measurements for depth can be found by taking half the span (or length) of the beam in feet, calling it inches and adding an inch for good measure, i.e.:

14 ft. span: Depth $= 14/2 + 1 = 7 + 1 = 8$ in.

Such measurements, of course, are only approximate, depending on the nature of the load, and they can be reduced a little for steel.

Adjacency

While the basic orientation of the rooms is being considered, the question of adjacency—or what room goes next to which—must also be decided.

Here, the previously mentioned breakdown of rooms and spaces into the categories of living, utility, storage, and circulation will help. The category of living, which loosely included most of the principal rooms of the house, is now further broken down into the separate functions of living, eating, and sleeping. Obviously, the sleeping function should be separated from the others for privacy and quiet and therefore, ideally, bedrooms and bathroom should form a self-contained group. It should not be necessary, for instance, to cross a living room to get from a bedroom to the bathroom. (Children, of course, find it entertaining to do this when there are evening guests in, but invalids or early-bedders do not!) Having bedrooms that open onto the living room, therefore, should be avoided when possible. There are times when this arrangement may be necessary as a way of saving space by eliminating long corridors, and indeed it is common practice in new building in many countries, including Sweden, where space is at a premium; the price, however, is lack of privacy—also at a premium. (Frequently, of course, that little room which opens off the living room and which defies all efforts to be grouped with the rest of the bedrooms, though labeled "study" or just "room" on the plan, somehow ends up being used as a bedroom without any great inconvenience to anyone.)

The functions of living and eating, on the other hand, are not mutually exclusive and need not be entirely separated. It is now common practice to replace the traditional dining room with a dining space within, or connected to, the main living area. This arrangement gives a greater feeling of spaciousness when space is scarce and there are still many ways to screen off this area to a greater or lesser extent without using a partition if complete openness is not desired. Some of these methods will be described in the next section, dealing with individual rooms and spaces.

Wherever the dining area or dining room is, however, it must never be far from the kitchen. For ease of service, the two should be adjacent whenever possible, with perhaps a serving hatch or open counter between them. Many of the old houses were designed to be run by servants and no great effort was made to eliminate work; often, in fact, there was an intentionally long distance between kitchen and dining room, one being the domain of the "staff" and the other of the family, so that considerable replanning is necessary for present-day needs.

So far, the placement of the main rooms and their grouping for convenience have been established. One can see that the rooms and spaces tend to divide into two distinct groups: the living-eating-kitchen group and the bedroom-bathroom group. If there is no separate provision for toilet facilities near the living area, the bathroom will also have to be conveniently located near it—if possible so that it can be reached without having to pass too many bedroom doors.

If a diagram was to be drawn at this point, it would look like this.

It might be translated into the earlier layouts as shown in Figures 1 and 2 on page 131.

Economy

At this point, however, the factor of cost again enters the scene and may determine just how far we can proceed with our original decisions. Assuming that our money is limited, as in most cases, we must next examine an "invisible" element of building which is relatively expensive and often needlessly so—the plumbing—to see how it fits in with our ideal layout.

There are three simple rules for keeping plumbing costs down:

1) Have as few pipes as possible.
2) Keep them as short as possible.
3) Bend them as little as possible.

One of the more expensive items is the stack, or vertical pipe into which the fixtures discharge. This usually rises the whole height of the house and ends at a point above the roof where it is vented to the open air. If the plumbing fixtures are scattered all over the house, several stacks will be necessary whereas if the plumbing is centralized several fixtures can share the same stack, thus saving a considerable amount of money. What this means in simple terms is that in a bathroom, the fixtures should be kept as much as possible on one wall—called the "wet wall" or chase—which contains all the necessary vertical pipes; if there is a kitchen, another bathroom, or just plumbing on the same floor, it should, if possible, be placed back-to-back with the chase or adjacent, so that they may share the same stacks and pipes in a common "wet wall"; other bathrooms, kitchens, and so forth on other floors should be located so that they are on or near the "wet wall," which should rise vertically through the building shifting its location as little as possible.

In order to take advantage of plumbing economy, the adjacency diagram will now have to be modified as shown.

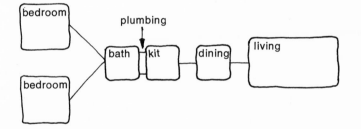

This could be translated into a layout similar to Figure 2 on page 170, where the kitchen and bathroom both share the same stacks.

Perfect centralization of pipes is, of course, an ideal not always possible in rehab work, and compromises have to be made. Often "wet walls" won't line up exactly on different floors, for instance, or an extra stack may be needed for a small toilet somewhere that refuses to line up with anything on the other floors. On the other hand, the ideal layout may have to be modified considerably in order to simplify the plumbing. How far general convenience and layout logic can be sacrificed to plumbing economy is a matter between the owner and his budget, and cannot be generalized on here. It can only be said that the best layout plan is the one that solves most of the problems, including that of cost.

At this point, it might be helpful to summarize some of the items that have been discussed in the form of a checklist of questions.

Checklist of questions on the general layout

1. Which rooms need daylight most?
   (This is where windows are limited, as in a row house.)
2. Which rooms need direct sunlight most?
3. Which is the best side of the house for the living room?
   (I.e., view of street versus access to garden, special view.)
4. Where can a large space such as the living room be most conveniently located with the minimum removal of structural walls?
5. Is it possible to go from the bedrooms to a bathroom without passing through a living area?
6. Are the toilet facilities convenient to the living area?
7. Is the dining area to be open or enclosed?
8. Are there more plumbing stacks than necessary?
9. Is there adequate provision for acoustical privacy in the living areas?
10. Are the sizes of the rooms proportionate to their importance and use?
11. Do corridors and stairs take too much space from the living areas?

The Open Plan

Before going in detail into the needs of the various rooms and spaces, it might be appropriate to say a few words about the philosophy of the open plan and its implications.

One of the major contributions of twentieth-century architecture was its reawakening of interest in the use of space for its own sake—particularly in houses and smaller buildings. This may have happened, at first, by way of compensation for the removal of nearly all the decorative interest of the previous era, or perhaps for the reduction in ceiling heights and general scale that has already been noted, but for whatever reason, internal partitions began to disappear about the 1920's in many of the more advanced designs, until the whole house tended to become one space or a series of interconnecting spaces. The bathroom remained inviolate, but even the bedroom would be replaced on occasion by a semi-private sleeping balcony opening into the main living area in an effort to gain maximum spatial unity.

Such interior layouts were, of course, rather extreme and suited only to a particular life style (which presumably excluded children), but the idea of opening up space was attractive and all sorts of modified forms of the open plan became common currency—so much so that today many dwellings tend to suffer from a lack of privacy. Many people (including the writer) are no doubt familiar with the problem of trying to escape from the sound of a television set in an open plan house, for instance; there is simply no solution other than retiring to a bedroom and/or wearing earplugs! Devices such as the hi-fi headphone have made it

143

possible to listen to music regardless of other sounds, but in the long run there is no substitute for a certain degree of built-in privacy in the house itself.

These remarks are not intended to discourage the use of open planning, however—merely to warn against the side effects of its over-use. The extent to which a plan can be opened up obviously will depend on the tastes of the owner, the number of people living in the house, and the similarity and diversity of their interests.

In addition to the removal of walls, interesting spaces can also result from the removal of the whole or part of a floor or ceiling at just the right place—provided that it is structurally feasible to do so. This should never be done just because it is a "new idea," however, and the whole room must be visualized and planned for furniture so that the ceiling does not rise at some arbitrary point unrelated to the whole layout.

No

The same applies even more when dropping part of a floor—which is also possible—since this creates not only a spatial but also a physical division in the room. Even one little step has the effect of dividing the area into two parts, each of which has its own function and layout of furniture.

Needless to say, a step, or steps, should be introduced only if there is enough space and if they fit logically into the layout (i.e., stepping down into the living area from the dining area); otherwise they can be a nuisance and a hazard.

When introducing steps or a small change in floor level, what happens to the ceiling in the room beneath must also be considered. If part of the floor is being lowered there will be a corresponding drop in the level of the ceiling underneath (Figure 1 below); this can be concealed by a change of use in the lower floor as in Figure 2, or, if there is enough spare height, by a hung ceiling as in Figure 3.

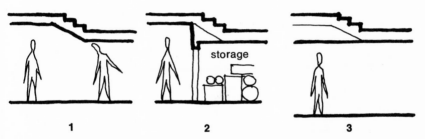

storage

1   **2**   **3**

Lowering floors, however, tends to be expensive and is usually done only when it is necessary to rebuild the whole floor structure for some other reason. A similar effect to Figure 3 above can sometimes be achieved without removing the existing floor, by building *up* from it to establish the higher level. If the higher levels are above or near the sill height of the existing windows, of course, they must be kept away from outer walls to avoid rebuilding the windows and altering the outside appearance of the house—unless this is desired.

This technique can be most useful when converting high-ceilinged spaces with concrete floors into apartments. By raising the floor level of all the internal accommodation, including the corridor and entrance hall, it is then possible to step *down* into the living area and other important spaces without having to smash through solid concrete.

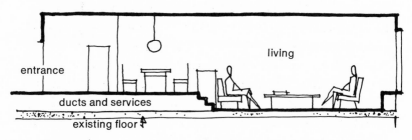

The space under the built-up floors is also convenient for concealing air ducts, plumbing, wiring, and so forth.

The double-story space can be a very effective way of giving an exciting new dimension to a rather conventional interior. Again, it must be used wisely and not just because it is an "idea." If the proposal is to walk down into the space, for example, the location of the new stairs must relate to the new layout of the room so that the room can be furnished properly. (This can be tested with a rough model such as described in the next chapter.) Also, the removal of large areas of structural floor may cause the outer walls of the house to buckle or even collapse for lack of horizontal bracing.

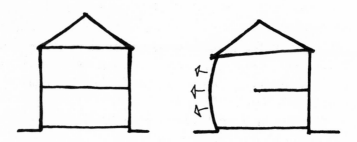

The wall construction should therefore be checked by an architect, engineer, or competent builder before floors are removed.

Lastly, there is the esthetic, and sometimes structural, problem of how to treat the old windows in the new two-story space. The arrangement shown in Figure 1 below is typical, with the old windows untouched but now floating around awkwardly in a large wall and still expressing the idea of two separate floors—except, of course, that the upper ones are now beyond human reach for purposes of opening and closing.

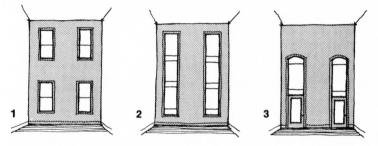

Figure 2 shows an attempt to express the idea of a double-story space by removing some of the brickwork and uniting the windows in single vertical apertures. Sometimes this also looks awkward because of the excessive height of the opening and the consequent weakening of the wall (which again should be checked by a competent structural authority), so that it may be necessary to lower the head, as in Figure 3, to get the desired proportion. The extra cost of lowering the head may be money well spent for a good purpose—both esthetically and structurally—provided that the result also relates well to the *outside* appearance of the house.

IX

The Interior: Planning the Rooms and Spaces

By this time the reader is familiar with the varied and often conflicting needs that help determine the location of the principal rooms and spaces. It remains now to discuss in more detail the needs of the rooms and spaces themselves.

By adhering to the local building laws (which are mandatory at all times) and to the recommendations in the Building Planning Section of HUD's manual PG-50 (see Appendix B), which are mandatory if federal funds are used, one can be sure that the rooms and spaces are *big* enough and are properly lighted and ventilated. One cannot, however, as the Guide points out, be sure that they will be *conveniently shaped* for the needs of living and the proper location of furniture. To quote a simple instance, the bedroom shown in Figure 1 opposite has adequate floor area, a simple, straightforward shape, and good lighting, but it has one fault—there is no place to put a bed!

By simply moving the door, however, as in Figure 2, the room becomes *livable*.

This example may be extreme, but how many bedrooms can one think of where there is no convenient place for, say, a chest of drawers or a dressing table? Adequate area,

1   **2**

light, and ventilation don't necessarily make a livable room.

The *livability* of a remodeled room or space is largely determined by three factors: 1. its size; 2. its shape; 3. the location and size of existing fixed features, such as windows, doors, radiators, fireplaces, flues, etc.

Although the size of a room may be enforceable by law, the question of shape—for better or for worse—eludes legislation. Thus it is possible to do almost anything with internal partitions provided there is the money to pay for it, and one of the most common—and expensive—characteristics of bad layout plans is the partition that "jogs" or bends at the slightest provocation, and *always* at the wrong place. Compare the relative livability, for instance, of the following layouts, all of which have the same floor area.

✳ bottleneck

The rule, therefore, is to *keep the room shapes as simple as possible*—they look better, give a greater feeling of space, are furnished and cleaned more easily, and usually are more economical to construct.

Existing features, such as windows, doors, radiators, fireplaces, flues, and so forth, which are normally encountered in rehab work, can be a help or a hindrance to the layout, and decisions have to be made whether to eliminate or incorporate them. Obviously, if a substantial feature such as an unused fireplace or chimney stack, which would be expensive to demolish, can be retained or turned to good account in the new layout, it is money saved for other purposes.

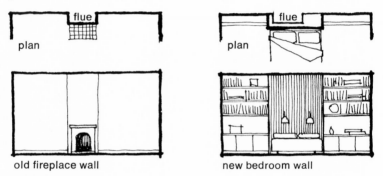

old fireplace wall   new bedroom wall

NOTE: Before attempting to open up an old fireplace for use with wood fires, be sure that the flue connecting it to the open air above is unobstructed, in good condition, and *is adequate for the purpose.* Many flues were originally constructed to be used only as hot-air ducts from the basement or as vents for gas fires, and will not withstand the heat from a wood fire. *It can be dangerous not to get professional advice on this point.*

Doors, on the other hand, can be blocked up and relocated relatively easily if necessary for a better room layout, as in the bedroom example already illustrated. If there are special moldings or architectural detail on the door frame that match similar details in the rest of the room they should be carefully removed and reinstalled on the new frame. Also, the new door location must make esthetic sense as well as contribute to the workability of the room.

The window openings are less flexible, and alterations here can be costly—especially if in a brick or stone wall. Therefore, unless there is a really good reason for change—such as the creation of a double-story space as described in the last chapter—they are best left alone. Certain changes of design are possible *within* the total opening of course—for instance, a new type of window can be installed—but very careful thought must be given to such a change, since the external appearance of the house may be adversely affected. Also, the practice of partially blocking up a window opening to raise the sill height or lower the height of the lintel can ruin the outside appearance of the house (even if the new material merges invisibly with the surrounding wall), and it should therefore be avoided—especially on the more important sides of the house.

Many of these problems concerning fixed features, however—including radiators—will be dealt with more fully when interior and exterior details are discussed.

As implied, the final test of a livable room is the extent to which the furniture or appliances fit within it to create the greatest sense of comfort and space for the occupants. This most important part of design is so often overlooked or avoided—even by architects—that some special consideration must be given to it here. Therefore, the rest of this chapter will describe in some detail the needs of each room or space and the ways storage and circulation elements relate to them.

Kitchens

Since kitchens have more specific requirements than many of the other spaces, it would be appropriate to begin with them.

The three main centers of activity in a kitchen are the sink, the stove, and the refrigerator, and if a triangle is drawn between them the sides will represent the paths most often taken by the person cooking. This is known as the "work triangle," and it can give an indication of the efficiency of the layout. It is shown shaded in each of the following diagrams.

There are, broadly speaking, four distinct types of layout.

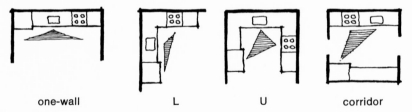

one-wall   L   U   corridor

In the compact working-kitchen all four are commonly used, but in the larger dining-kitchen the "U" and "corridor" are less suitable because of the extreme length or extreme separation of the work areas.

It is not possible in the scope of this book to analyze the dozens of variations of the four basic layouts that can be used in specific situations, but for those interested the University of Illinois Small Homes Council has published a *Kitchen Planning Guide* that does just this. It also recommends that the sum of the *sides* of the work triangle should not exceed twenty-six feet and be preferably less than twenty-three feet; this, however, applies mainly to the larger kitchen or dining-kitchen with larger counters.

It will be seen that in both the "L" and "U" plans the counter has to turn corners, which creates a problem of access to the storage underneath. This can only be solved by having a large, deep, irregularly shaped compartment with a small door, perhaps at a forty-five-degree angle, or by using a revolving "lazy Susan."

Neither is entirely satisfactory, so in the smaller kitchen (when space is not too tight), a modified "corridor"-type layout is often used (with only one door), instead of the "L" or "U" types.

One of the vital dimensions in all small kitchens should be mentioned: that between the fronts of parallel counter cabinets in a "U" or "corridor" layout, or between the front of a counter cabinet and a wall in a "one wall" or "L" layout. This should generally not be less than four feet—especially if there is a low-level oven.

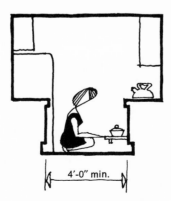

4'-0" min.

The face of the cabinets is normally two feet (or twenty-four inches) from the face of the wall with a twenty-five-inch counter projecting one inch beyond it.

When planning the kitchen, one of the first essentials is continuity in the counters, and it is precisely when trying to achieve this that the existing fixed features such as windows, doors, and flues seem to get most in the way. If the kitchen is located in the center of the apartment or house away from windows for reasons of plumbing economy (see Chapter VIII, page 141), the designer has a clean slate, as it were, but otherwise the layout is liable to get cut up somewhat by doors and windows and existing jogs and projections. Doors, as already noted, are relatively easy to move, but windows often pose certain problems because of their sill height. This is usually around two feet six inches off the floor, whereas a kitchen counter top is up at three feet, so that short of building up the windows, with possible unfortunate repercussions on the outside of the building, the only course of action is to stop the counter top at the window. In the larger dining-kitchen the problem can be solved by having the dining area next to the window, or windows, thus keeping the counter tops off the outside wall, as in Figure 1 below, but in the compact working-kitchen this may not be so easy. The modified "corridor" plan (with only one door), however, often saves the day in such a situation, as in Figure 2 below.

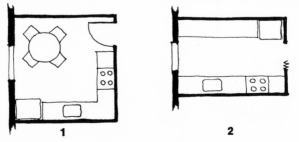

1   **2**

Sometimes a window is located so near the side wall that the end of a counter top will cover part of it. In addition to being awkward to construct (and possibly unhygienic by creating uncleanable crevices for food to fall into), such a situation is unsightly both from the outside and the inside. Better in this case to leave a space between the end of the counter and the window that can be used to accommodate, for instance, a rubber plant or a small trash can.

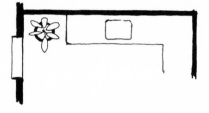

(This arrangement also, incidentally, solves the problem of fitting a series of kitchen units of standard dimensions into a room of fixed length without "padding.")

Another interrupter of counter continuity is the family-size refrigerator—the skyscraper of the kitchen landscape. It need hardly be said that this should be located at the end of the counter whenever possible and *not* in the middle as is too often seen.

The stove, incidentally, should not be located near windows—especially where there are drapes that may blow over it and catch fire. Furthermore the flame in a gas burner in such a situation can be blown out with dangerous results.

It is customary, of course, to have an upper tier of cupboards over the working counter top, and these can cause certain problems in layouts that are otherwise good. Generally speaking, the cupboards can start at a height of fifteen to eighteen inches above the working top (4'-3" to 4'-6" from the floor) and should be as continuous and regular as possible. However, they must:

1. stop at a window
2. jump up to twenty-two inches over a sink
3. jump up to thirty inches over a stove (so that they and their contents will not get toasted)
4. jump up to thirty inches above counter height over a family-size refrigerator.

These varying heights can make the cupboards resemble an inverted Manhattan skyline, so care must be given to the placing of the above-mentioned elements and perhaps of the counters themselves.

In some cases a particular location of "immovables" such as windows and doors may make it impossible ideally to locate both the counter and the overhead cabinets, and some compromise has to be made—usually at the expense of cupboard continuity. In all cases, however, the recommendation of HUD's rehabilitation guide (HUD's manual PG-50) on minimum acceptable footage of shelving should be adhered to.

Generally, the most serious fault in rehab kitchen layouts is lack of continuity in the working area—Figure 1 below shows an all-too-typical situation. With a little bit of perseverance, however, it is often not too difficult to come up with something better, as in Figure 2, without straining the budget.

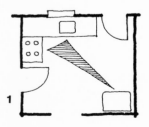 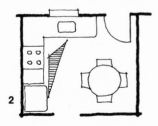

In certain cases—such as small apartments—a kitchen would take up a disproportionate amount of the available space and therefore a kitchenette unit is appropriate. It is usually of the "one wall" layout and is ideally located in a special alcove so that it can be shut off from the rest of the room when not in use.

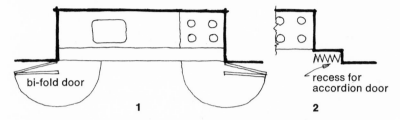

The alcove can be as deep as the rest of the plan will permit but must at least be the width of the counter (25″) plus a few inches to allow for the folding doors and a little space between them and the cabinet front when closed. "Bi-fold" doors as shown in Figure 1 above do not project into the alcove opening when in the open position but folding accordion doors such as shown in Figure 2 take up quite a bit of alcove space when in the folded position, and this must be allowed for so that the drawers and doors of the kitchenette unit can open properly.

Bathrooms

Although the requirements are as specific as those of kitchens, bathroom layouts usually do not pose quite so many problems. Because of the number of plumbing fixtures, however, some attention must be given to economy and an effort made to locate these fixtures on the same wall—the "wet wall" referred to on page 141. If this wall can be backed up to the kitchen, so much the better.

As in the kitchen, existing windows can give trouble, the only difference here being that bathroom windows are usually tucked away at the back of the house and (if not already different in proportion from the other windows), can often have their sills raised without causing notice.

However, a bath, for instance, should not be located under a window—however high the sill—for four good reasons:

1. Excessive moisture from condensing steam or showers will cause the window frame and finish to deteriorate.
2. It is necessary to provide an extra waterproof curtain for it if the bath is used also as a shower.
3. Unpleasant cold down-drafts are caused in the wintertime.
4. The window is more difficult to operate because of the tub being in the way.

The bathtub is best located so that it is enclosed on three sides either by the walls of the bathroom or by an alcove. This arrangement keeps the shower curtain or screen system simple and eliminates those awkward left-over spaces at the end of the tub that were characteristic of many older bathrooms.

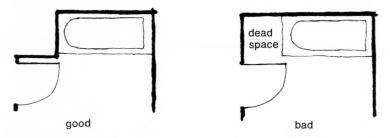

Finding the best relationship between the basin and the window can be difficult. One of the best solutions (from an interior point of view at least) is to have a long clerestory window with a sill height of about five feet from the floor, under which the sink and mirror can be accommodated. This gives light from the best direction for shaving—head on. If a high sill is not possible or will spoil the outside appearance of the house, a good alternative is to have the sink near the window but on a wall at right angles to it.

Having the sink or sinks set in a continuous counter top is now standard practice but does require more space than the minimal five feet by seven feet compartment one has to adopt occasionally in rehabilitation work.

The toilet should be located next to the bathtub, plumbing economy permitting, so that when the top is down it serves as a useful seat when washing children in the bath, and so forth—a point often overlooked in planning.

The bidet, if used, should be located near the toilet and bathtub.

One of the most common faults in bad remodeling layouts is the irregularly shaped bathroom with scattered plumbing fixtures, and it may well be worth the cost of moving a few small partitions to get a better and more economical layout such as in Figure 2 below—one of the simplest and best layouts for general use.

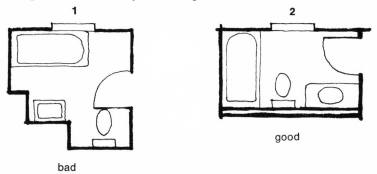

1

2

bad

good

In the "bad" figure, not only is the bathtub directly under the window but also the doorswing almost hits both the toilet and the sink—an arrangement both inconvenient and potentially hazardous. (In an extreme case, such as an elderly person collapsing while using the sink or the toilet, it might be impossible to open the door.) Such layouts, as well as being awkward to use and to plumb are more difficult to clean and often waste money in the *building* of unnecessary jogs in new partitions. In nearly all cases they can be improved with a little thought and planning skill.

Bedrooms

The Building Planning Section of HUD's manual PG-50 gives minimum floor areas for different types of bedroom and also minimum sizes for the smallest dimension of the room—the latter ensuring that there is enough space to get past the bed.

To avoid drafts, the bed or beds should not, if possible, be located between a window and a door and should *never* be located at or under a window. At least one wall of the room, therefore, must be kept free of doors and windows so that the bed or beds can go against it if one is to avoid the situation shown on page 149—and this wall must be of sufficient length to allow for bedside tables or chairs and sufficient access space. Here are two typical instances.

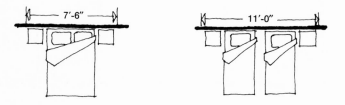

The clothes closet, and its correct location, is one of the most important elements in a bedroom and one most often overlooked or added as an apparent afterthought. First, it must be big enough: a *clear* two feet in depth for proper hanging of clothes and as long as convenient, allowing at least two feet per person. Second, it should be built *in* and not *out* (as in the "afterthought" variety); the built-out closet is a common cause of unnecessary jogs in badly laid out bedrooms and—like the obsolete wardrobe—can create bottlenecks in the circulation.

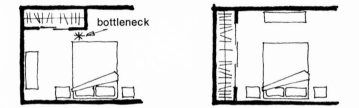

Third, the closet should have some space in front of it and should, if possible, be related to the dressing table and chest of drawers so that together they form a dressing area. Space permitting, this can also be in a separate alcove or small room opening off the main bedroom.

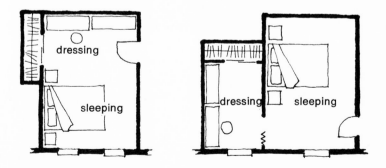

Fourth, closets have an important incidental function that should be stressed—they form excellent sound buffers between rooms. Through proper planning it is often possible to take advantage of this fact and still have them suitably located in the bedrooms. They will be of most use between bedrooms, between bedrooms and bathrooms, and between bedrooms and living rooms, in that order, and every effort should be made to locate them in these positions providing that the bedroom layout does not suffer in consequence. Here are some typical situations.

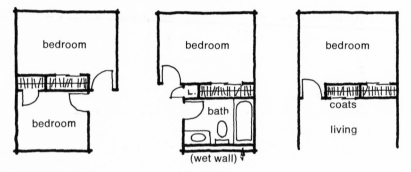

Living Spaces

It remains now to say a few words about those most important areas of the house that are used for the various waking activities: relaxation, conversation, entertaining, eating, reading, playing a musical instrument, television watching, sewing, hi-fi listening, writing, etc. Needless to say, if all or even some of these activities were to go on in the same space, bedlam would ensue (as mentioned apropos of privacy and the open plan on page 143), so one of the aims in planning must be to try to arrange things so that the number of potential collision courses is kept to a minimum.

In the average remodeling situation with medium to small existing rooms, one should aim for the maximum amount of openness in the living spaces, consistent with the legitimate needs of privacy and—of course—cost.

Where there can be only one living area due to lack of space, conflicting activities can, of course, only be separated by timing them so as not to overlap and by using the bedroom, say, for clarinet practice. Otherwise, where more space is available, some of the more permanently noisy activities such as children's T.V. watching should be conveniently located in an enclosed space. Activities that are compatible, on the other hand, such as relaxation, conversation, eating, and entertaining, really do not need any space division, so certain walls can be removed if desired—say, between an existing dining room and living room—if it is structurally feasible to do so.

Proportion again may have a say here—this time in determining the relative sizes of the spaces—as it is always more restful, visually and psychologically, to have a dominating space with smaller related spaces rather than a series of almost equal compartments.

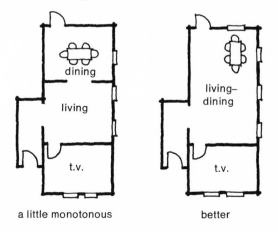

a little monotonous   better

The final test of the living spaces will be how well they permit the furniture to be grouped and arranged attractively for maximum convenience in the fullest sense of the word; therefore no decisions about removing or relocating walls or doors should be made until this aspect has been explored thoroughly. Failure to do this can result in time and money being wasted.

For those unaccustomed to drawing or thinking on paper, the best way to study the possibilities of furniture layout is to draw a simple outline of the room or space to a scale of one fourth of an inch to the foot and show all features, such as doors, windows, radiators, fireplaces, flues, and jogs in the partitions. Next, cut out of thin cardboard the outline (seen from above) of standard items of furniture such as chairs, sofas, tables, bookcases, and specific items necessary. These can then be pushed around the plan and the effects of different groupings and the possible removal of certain partitions can be studied with none of the inconvenience and cost that would arise from doing it at full scale.

This game of cardboard furnishing, of course, can also be played with bedrooms and any space where there is a choice to be made in the location of standard units. On the opposite page is a graphic list of some typical units drawn to a scale of three sixteenths of an inch to the foot, which can be traced onto cardboard and cut out for use as "pawns" —just make sure they represent the same size as the actual units to be used. For those interested, further variations or refinements are possible, such as using the larger scale of one half of an inch to the foot, making three-dimensional furniture models, building up the walls, and so forth. It is also possible, when using the flat cardboard pieces, to affix small bits of magnetic tape to the backs so that they will

STANDARD FURNITURE (scale: $\frac{3}{16}'' = 1'\text{-}0''$)

Living/Dining

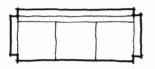

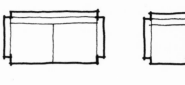

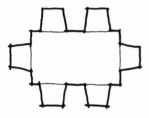

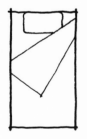

Sleeping:

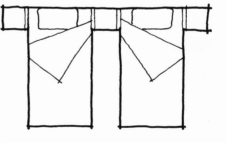

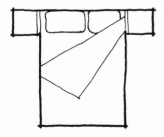

Feet:

| 0 | 5 | 10 |

adhere to a metal chalk board on which the room outline can be drawn or to which the drawing can be taped.

Many living spaces suffer from the lack of a main focus of interest. Before the era of the radiator and central heating there was no such problem, the sitting area being necessarily centered around the fireplace, which expressed its importance in terms of ornate mantelpieces, mirrors, shelves, symmetrical arrangements of urns and other objets d'art. Most of the recreational interests of the household were confined to this area—especially in winter. With the break-up of the hearth, as it were, by the introduction of uniform heat throughout the house, activities have become more dispersed and technologically sophisticated, so that now there are such centers of interest as the television, the hi-fi, and the coffee table—all rather poor visual substitutes for the open fireplace with its continuous drama of changing shapes and lights. (The electric "log" fire is, of course, an admission of this fact and only a partially successful attempt to regain some of the atmosphere of a real fire.)

Arranging furniture in the absence of a strong unifying element such as a fireplace, then, can pose many problems if one wants the room to look restful and attractive as well as being tailored to the needs of the occupants. These can often be solved by arranging the furniture in groups rather than as individual isolated pieces as was common in the past. A couch in a sitting area, for instance, may be backed up to a chest of drawers in the dining area, thereby defining the two areas without actually dividing them from each other. Many other combinations are possible, both side by side and back to back, using either standard furniture units such as bookcases or cabinets or special built-in or built-out units made for the room.

166

The diagrams on the following page illustrate three different furniture layouts arising from three different ways of remodeling the same space. The first shows the traditional living room with the furniture arranged symmetrically around the fireplace—obviously the choice for those intending to restore an interesting old room to something like its original appearance. To do this successfully, of course, most of the original details must be there—cornices, moldings, paneled doors—and these will be discussed in the next chapter. (It will be noted that the original dining room arrangement has been kept, since the removal of a wall would break the continuity of the ceiling cornice.) Where the original details are in bad shape or the owner wants a modern interior anyway, and the fireplace is to remain, the second layout would be appropriate. The wall between the dining and living rooms has been removed to create one large space and the sitting area arranged asymmetrically and more casually around the fireplace. It will be noted that the dining and living functions are defined by the use of one of the furniture groupings already described. In the third layout—also a modern one—space is at a premium and the fireplace has been sealed up to permit more freedom of furniture arrangement. Again the grouping of the pieces defines the different functions of eating and general living. This type of layout might be found in a small apartment, with the T.V. or hi-fi on the shelves to the right of the living area.

A good final test for a planned layout is to draw a circulation profile of the whole space. This can be done simply by tracing the "coastline" formed by the walls and furniture around the room, with free standing pieces in the room as islands or peninsulas. The resulting "sea" will then take the exact shape of the combined living and circulation

1

2

3

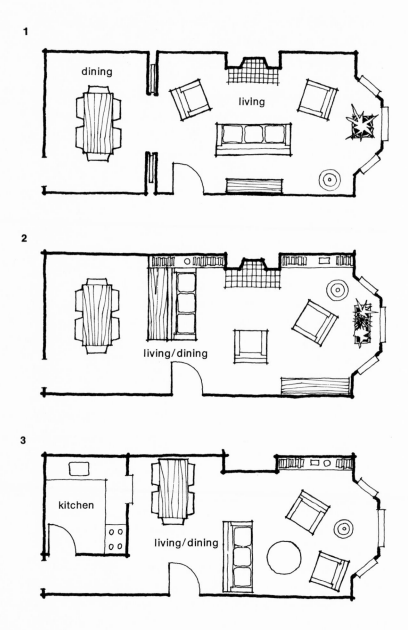

spaces defined by the placing of the furniture. In this way
any bottlenecks or underused spaces can quickly be de-
tected and, hopefully, eliminated.

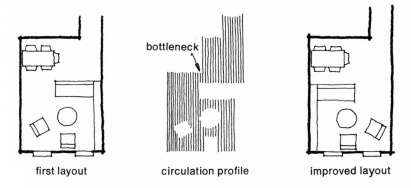

first layout   circulation profile   improved layout

When everything works to satisfaction in the living
areas, the plan can then begin to be finalized once one last
item in the house or apartment has been checked—the general circulation.

Circulation

In addition to those parts of the rooms already mentioned that enable people to move around, the
general circulation of the house or apartment includes those
elements of the layout that connect the rooms and spaces
together—halls, corridors, and stairs. In apartment buildings or condominiums, there is a further distinction between public circulation, which is used by all occupants,
and private circulation, which is within the apartments
themselves; and the use of certain details that may be
slightly hazardous—such as winders or spiral staircases—is
usually prohibited by local building laws in the public circulation but not in the private circulation (on the theory,

no doubt, that the occupant's apartment is his castle and he therefore takes his own risks!).

The efficiency of the layout of a house or apartment can often be judged by the shape of the general circulation—which can be seen by drawing a circulation profile as described in the last section—and by the amount of area it occupies in relation to other rooms and spaces. Part of the charm of many old houses, of course, is the spaciousness of the halls, corridors, staircases, and landings, but these are usually in suitable proportion to the rooms in the rest of the house. Where space is scarce in a remodeling situation, the circulation should be reduced proportionately so that valuable living space is not lost.

No   **Yes**

The corridor in the first layout above, for example, is unnecessarily long, has many corners to clean, and has no natural light, whereas in the second layout it is short, simple, and gets some light from the living room. The area of corridor eliminated is also plowed back in the form of extra living room space.

In addition to being short and simple, corridors and halls should be adequately wide and be free of "bottle-necks" so that furniture (and people) can move easily.

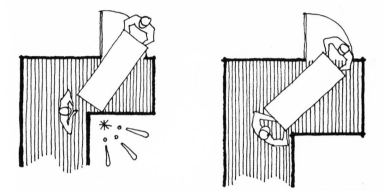

To avoid the familiar calamity depicted in the first sketch above, which seems to happen whenever furniture is moved, all corridors—including the small "dog leg" part, which is giving the trouble here—should be at least 3'-3" to 3'-6" wide at all points. In tight situations, or where an existing corridor is to be reused, a width of 3'-0" is acceptable.

The coat closet, which has so far not been specifically mentioned, should of course be located in the circulation somewhere convenient to the entrance door of the house or apartment. It is very often overlooked and has to be forced in somewhere at the last minute, usually at the expense of some other part of the layout. Similarly to bedroom closets, it should have a clear depth of two feet and be as long as convenient.

When planning stairs, bottlenecks should also be avoided. These often take the form of a too-narrow landing.

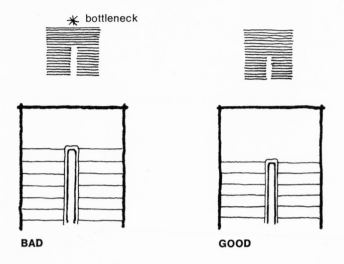

BAD **GOOD**

Needless to say, a narrow landing is illogical and inconvenient. A landing must be at *least* as wide as the stairs.

Spiral staircases are extremely attractive and very useful in certain situations where a conventional staircase would take up too much room. They are best located in a large two-story space where they can be seen to best advantage—and near a convenient corner or wall so that they don't cut up the floor space unnecessarily. If possible, however, they should not be depended on as the sole means of vertical access to, say, a bedroom floor, because of the difficulty in moving heavy furniture and a certain element of hazard they may present to the very old and the very young due to the tapered treads. Care should also be taken to see that the first or the last treads at each floor are facing in an appropriate direction—a point often overlooked when planning on paper.

X

The Interior: Special Details, Features, and Finishes

There are, of course, many valid paths toward rehabilitation, and this applies perhaps even more to the interior treatment of a building than to the outside. It is important, therefore, that before anything is done to the interior, one should decide which of these paths is to be taken, or, in other words, what one wants it to *look* like. As with the exterior, the choices range from a complete restoration of the original through the something-old-something-new approaches to a completely modern interior that may contrast with the outside of the house. The two sketches on the following page are based on two of the plans shown on page 168 and illustrate, in terms of style, what can be done at either end of the spectrum with the same living space.

The choice of approach is basic and can depend on many factors, including how attractive the original rooms were, how much of the detail such as cornices and moldings survives in good or repairable condition, what sort of furniture the owner has or likes and, last but not least, what

his attitude is to modern architecture. Some of the possibilities might be:

1. Complete restoration of the whole interior with the appropriate furniture from the same period (modern kitchen and bathroom usually).

2. Complete restoration of certain rooms such as the living room with the rest of the house in simpler but harmonious style.

3. Original "fixed" details such as cornices, moldings, and paneled doors kept, contrasting with modern furniture and modern detailing on certain added "moveable" items such as shelves and cabinets.

4. Complete redesign of whole interior with modern detailing and furniture.

There are all kinds of possibilities of contrasting or harmonizing the old and the new—just as it is possible to mix genuine antique pieces successfully with modern furniture —and there can be no firm rules as to which is good or bad. Here the owner can "let himself go" more freely than on the exterior of the building (which has to relate to other buildings and to the general environment) and almost anything is acceptable *if done well.*

At this point some of the features and details commonly found in an old house should be discussed—those that, whether restored, altered, or removed, have a basic effect on the appearance of the interior. The last section will discuss appropriate finishes.

Features and Details

WALLS AND CEILINGS. Every effort should be made to preserve or repair existing details such as decorated ceilings, cornices, moldings, paneling; and window trim—

unless they are hopelessly ugly or decayed or cannot be accommodated in the design. Don't give up if parts of a cornice or molding are missing and it is no longer possible to buy matching items; it is often possible to build a close enough resemblance to an existing cornice by using stock moldings in combination or, if it is a molding that has to be matched, this can often be done simply by removing a piece of similar molding from a less important location in the house.

Any new layout of rooms should be designed so as to do the least damage to good existing detail. If, for instance, it is absolutely necessary to subdivide a living room that has a fine decorated ceiling and cornice, a full floor-to-ceiling partition such as shown in Figure 1 below should be avoided.

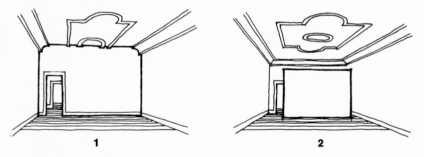

1   2

The continuity of the ceiling and cornice has been completely chopped up and no longer makes any sense. On the other hand, by selecting compatible uses for the subdivided spaces—such as living room and kitchenette, kitchen and dining area, or dining area and living room— the partition does not have to go right up to the ceiling or touch the walls, and such a "floating partition" will allow the ceiling, cornices, and any wall paneling or dado to run from one space to the other without interruption.

If the existing ceiling is in bad shape, it may be decided

to conceal it by applying a new ceiling underneath (Figure
1 below); if the cornice is also beyond repair, the new ceiling can be "hung" lower to conceal this too (Figure 2
below).

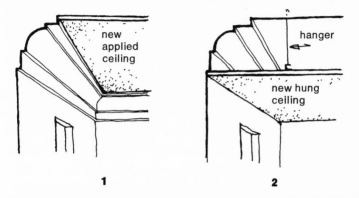

1   **2**

The hung ceiling can be useful also to conceal pipes in
bathrooms and kitchens, or to reduce the amount of space
in excessively high rooms—thereby reducing the heating
costs in the winter. It should not, however, be lowered beyond the top of the window trim or the continuity of the
"frame" around the window opening will be broken, as in
Figure 2 below.

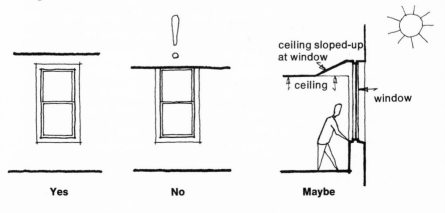

Occasionally, it is absolutely necessary for some reason to lower a ceiling below the level of the top of a window, and in this case part of the ceiling adjacent to the top of the window can be raised or sloped up, as in Figure 3 above, to form a kind of dormer or scuttle. The alternate solution of lowering the head of the windows by rebuilding nearly always spoils the appearance of the building from the outside and is most strongly *not recommended* without some advice from a competent architect.

While speaking of living room ceilings, a word must be said about the paneled or tiled types that have become popular. Many of these ceilings, though easily installed by the average handyman, unfortunately do not look well in old houses unless a completely modern interior is being planned. Generally, the larger the unit and the more pronounced the grid effect the less appropriate it looks with anything but flush doors and flat trim. Panel units—particularly with an exposed metal grid—may be appropriate in large office ceilings but do not belong in a house.

WINDOWS. Care should be taken when locating new partitions near window openings. If there is wood trim on the surface of the existing wall it should not be overlapped by the new partition or one gets the effect of an incomplete "picture frame," as in Figure 2 opposite. If the partition is kept at a respectful distance from the trim, as in Figure 1, the area will not only look better from the room but also give some space for drapes or curtains. One of the reasons for including a sketch and measurement of the window trim in a survey (as mentioned on pages 123–4) is to avoid such "accidents" when locating new partitions.

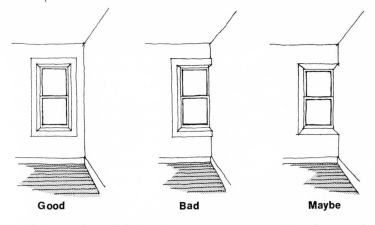

Good   **Bad**   **Maybe**

Often, when fighting for space on one side of a partition, it is necessary to push it as far as possible toward the window. If there is no wood trim the face of the wall can, in an emergency, be merged flush with the ingoing plaster face of the window opening, as in Figure 3 above.

DOORS. As with windows, care must be taken when locating new partitions near a door so that the trim is not disturbed. Doors, however, tend to give rise to other design problems not usually found when dealing with windows—probably because they are more often the subject of alteration.

The right type of door for a room is particularly important in rehabilitation work, where old and new must coexist harmoniously—often in the same room—and much money is frequently wasted in replacing good existing doors, which may only have needed to be scraped and painted, by something new of doubtful distinction. A few simple rules here may help eliminate some wrong choices:

   1. Good existing doors that match or harmonize with
      the general detailing of the room should be retained

and repaired if necessary—this applies particularly to rooms with cornices and door moldings in good condition (Figure 1 below).

2. Flush doors are appropriate when the detailing in the rest of the room is simple or has been replaced by modern treatment (Figure 2); in rooms that have more elaborate door moldings, however, flush doors sometimes look too bare and it is necessary to use some judgment that will take into account the color and texture of the door (Figures 3 and 4).

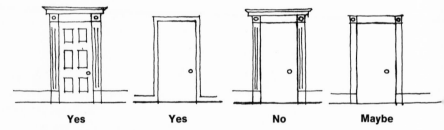

Yes   **Yes**   **No**   **Maybe**

3. Doors should not be replaced by replicas—either correct or incorrect—of doors from a period earlier than that of the house itself; the results are similar to implying distinguished ancestry by "name dropping."

4. For similar reasons, the use of false "panel" doors—which are obviously flush doors with moldings from the local lumber yard stuck on the surface—should be avoided; this time the ancestry is wholly imaginary!

Often the existing doors are in poor condition and anything like an accurate replica may prove to be too expensive. Here, it is best to use plain flush doors and keep the detailing in the rest of the room simple. Usually if the doors are in really bad shape the chances are that the other details will be in a similar state and can therefore be replaced with a simple modern treatment in keeping with the new flush doors.

When choosing new doors, some thought should also be given to the possible use of special door types for certain situations. In addition to the normal or side-hung door, there is also, for domestic work, the folding or accordion door, the double-hinged or bi-fold door, and the sliding door—with or without pocket.

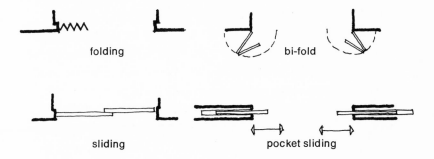

folding   bi-fold

sliding   pocket sliding

Folding doors, as well as making good dividers for large spaces, are useful in situations where a fully swinging door is impossible or undesirable, such as a coat closet in a narrow hall near the front door or in a kitchenette unit. They are also the stock-in-trade of the bad planner, who has failed to allow enough clearance for a doorswing in the bathroom, for instance. It is important to remember that in regular openings, a folding door will usually not shut off sound as well as a regular swinging door and therefore should not be used in bedrooms, bathrooms, television rooms, or where some degree of acoustical privacy is necessary. If it is impossible to use a regular door in such situations, there is usually something wrong with the layout.

It is also often forgotten that folding doors, when folded, still take up a considerable amount of space, and allowance must be made for it. In the case of a closet, this may not matter, but in a kitchenette unit, for instance, where the doors must clear the last drawer and cupboard, a solution such as described on page 157 must be adopted.

The bi-fold door has the advantage of simplicity and is particularly useful for kitchenette units, since it need not project into the opening at all when in the open position (unless the free end runs in a rail). It is also useful for bedroom closets and kitchens and there are some very attractive versions with simple louvers available.

Sliding doors are, of course, standard in clothes closets when the opening exceeds four feet across (under this width the doors become excessively narrow and do not slide as easily). The "pocket" version—where the door disappears into a slot in the wall when open—can also be useful for kitchens or other rooms when space is tight or an open door would get in the way. It should be remembered, however, that the thickness of the partition accommodating the pocket will be up around six inches instead of the normal four and three quarters and that this difference of width will usually have to be taken up on the kitchen side of the partition rather than outside, where it is more important that the wall be flush.

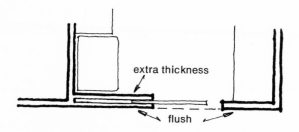

extra thickness

flush

RADIATORS. These fixtures were mentioned in the last chapter as being among the "fixed features" of a room—those items that may limit or suggest what can be done to the room. If a completely new heating system is being installed, of course, one can be more the master of one's destiny but where, as is often the case, existing radiators are to remain, they can cause unforeseen problems. If any remodeling is being done, it is very likely that one of the new partitions will come up against a radiator somewhere; and new drapes, for instance, might have to be made inelegantly short to avoid having them toasted by the radiator underneath the window! (Radiators are put under windows so they can heat the cold air that flows down off the glass in wintertime, but this arrangement is usually not reconcilable with floor-length drapes and is probably only justifiable in the case of large windows.)

If, as in many old houses, heat is conducted by a single pipe steam system, where one pipe comes up through the floor to connect to one end of the radiator, the radiator can be relocated to some extent simply by rotating it around the connection at the head of the upright pipe.

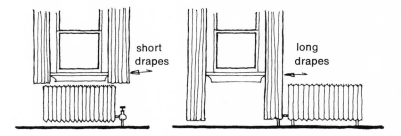

Swiveling is sometimes enough to get the radiator out of the way of a new partition or long drapes. In other cases, it is often well worth while to have some of the radiators completely relocated—perhaps on another wall of the room. In kitchens in particular, moving the radiators can often make the difference between a workable and unworkable layout.

Sometimes a radiator is well located but just looks a bit sad—and in this case some sort of enclosure may solve the problem. On the opposite page is shown a simple wooden cover that still expresses the idea of a radiator, allowing heat to circulate freely, while at the same time helping to relate it visually to the furniture of the room. The front is of ¾″ wide by 1½″ deep slats and the sides of the box are of ¾″ plywood; a ¼″ hardboard back gives the frame stability and ensures that the wall above does not become streaked from heat leaks. The slats are about 1″ apart and appear to float, but they are actually supported on two horizontal metal or ¾″ × 1½″ wood bars that run behind them and are painted dull black to be "invisible." The radiator should also be painted gray or black so that it will not be readily seen through the slats.

Similarly, radiators can often be enclosed as part of continuous wall-to-wall cabinet units in living rooms, bedrooms, and kitchens.

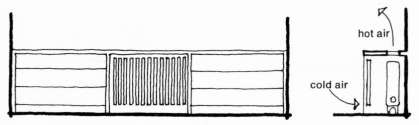

Care should be taken, however, that adequate provision is made to let the air circulate—the hot air rising freely from the radiator and cold air flowing in from floor level to replace it as shown in the figure above.

A RADIATOR COVER

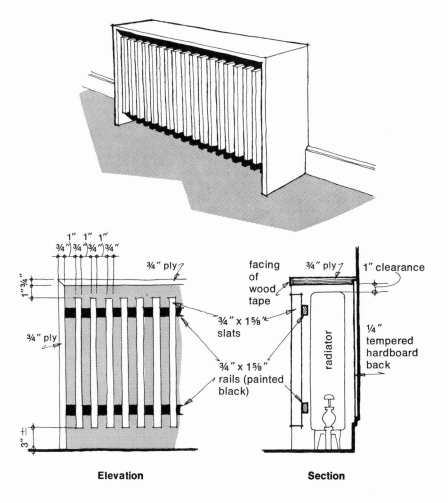

Elevation

Section

1" 1" 1"
¾" ¾" ¾" ¾"

¾" ply

1" ¾"

¾" ply

3" ±

facing of wood tape

¾" ply

1" clearance

¾" x 1⅝" slats

¾" x 1⅝" rails (painted black)

radiator

¼" tempered hardboard back

When relocating or replacing radiators on a one-pipe steam system, one should be sure that the bottom of the radiator slopes enough toward the pipe so that the condensed steam can flow back easily in the form of water.

This is particularly important in the case of long, slim radiators, which develop "water hammer" easily because of steam condensing too quickly in cold water lying at the foot of the radiator—the result being an alarming series of bangs.

STAIRS. The last details to be singled out for special mention are those connected with stairways. In old houses the stairway is often one of the most distinguished and attractive features, and every effort should be made to preserve it—if necessary by repairing or replacing damaged parts.

Often perfectly sound and elegant wooden rails and balustrades are taken out and replaced, in the name of "modernization," by easily obtainable "wrought iron" units. Such parts are neither genuinely traditional nor good modern design and look out of place in either context, appearing mean and skimpy against the sturdier detailing of the last century and ineffectively elaborate in a modern setting; they belong in fact to that architectural limbo already mentioned of things neither genuinely old nor new, and they should be given a wide berth by those seriously interested in design quality.

The selection of finishes and colors in a stairway is of special importance. Sometimes the beauty of the existing work is hidden by five coats of old paintwork (usually chocolate brown) and needs to be uncovered before its potentials are realized. A simple and effective new choice of colors—such as a black or natural wood finish for the handrail (both practical) and off-white balusters—can then transform a stairway into a thing of some elegance, even seeming to alter its proportions as in Figures 1 and 2 on the opposite page.

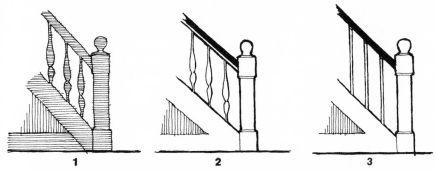

Generally the stairway is one of the areas where money can be saved and maximum design impact made by the proper application of sandpaper, paint, and imagination!

Even if the balusters are beyond repair, they can be replaced by suitably dimensioned wooden dowels, similar to broom handles—say ⅞″ to 1¼″ diameter in section, depending on how "heavy" the rest of the staircase looks. Where the handrail is also beyond repair, it can be replaced by a simple elliptical or round wooden section—say around 2″ in diameter. In either case, the newel posts (or heavy end balusters) should be left if some of the character of the original stairway is to be preserved (see Figure 3 above).

Finishes

The repair and improvement of the internal finishes of a house are aspects of rehabilitation that the average homeowner often feels tempted to do himself, either for personal satisfaction or in order to save money. If he is reasonably "handy" and goes about things the right way the results can be very rewarding on both counts and, in fact, he is often in the position of being able to lavish more time and care on the job than the average builder can and therefore may actually end up with what in some ways is a superior job. There are many books available for the handyman (some of which are mentioned in the bibliography) and it is not within the scope of this book to compete with them in detail. However, a few words can be said in the discussion of finishes about some of the processes and problems the "do-it-yourself" homeowner is likely to encounter.

REMOVING PAINT. Before refinishing woodwork it is often necessary to remove accumulated layers of old paint, and this process is not always easy—particularly if the paint is on molded paneling or elaborately carved balustrades. A good-quality paint remover, however, will usually do the job if applied generously and left on for the full recommended time. The paste form is more convenient than the liquid, since it does not run off vertical surfaces, and the nonflammable type is safest—although it must be used in a well-ventilated space. A stiff bristle brush is useful to ensure that the paste is forced into all the nooks and crannies where it is particularly needed and also that it comes out again with the dissolved paint. Other gadgets may also be helpful for getting paint out of tight corners—including dental instruments, which are particularly suitable for work on elaborate surfaces, being made of hard steel and designed for a somewhat similar purpose. In all cases, however, care must be taken not to damage the wood.

In an extreme situation where all methods have failed and the parts being treated are removable, they can be sent to a furniture-finishing workshop to be steeped in a large tank of special paint-removing fluid. This method would be especially appropriate when the wood has to be completely cleaned to take a clear natural finish.

PAINTING OVER WALLPAPER. While on the subject of paint, the question of whether or not to use it on top of the existing wallpaper is one that often arises. Obviously there is no standard answer, since well-applied wallpaper not more than ten years old, for instance, may be capable of supporting many coats of paint without anything happening to it, whereas if it *does* start to peel at some future date, the job of removing it may be a painful one, since most of the wallpaper-removing agents will not penetrate layers of paint. Where latex paint—which is relatively porous—has been used, the paper can sometimes be steamed off, but where oil-based paints have been used the only recourse may be to scrape everything off, bit by bit. All this can be simply summed up as follows: 1. if the existing wallpaper seems to be well hung and not brittle with age or about to peel off, latex paint can be used on it without too much element of risk; 2. do not use oil-based paint on wallpaper.

(In this respect the author must confess to having "lived dangerously" for many years by painting consistently over wallpaper and, despite gloomy prophecies, has never yet had to strip a wall—or move house quickly in order to avoid doing so . . .)

FLOOR FINISHES. When work is to be done on the floor, the question is often asked as to what type of finish is "correct" for a nineteenth-century house. Again, there can be no general answer, but in by far the greatest number of cases it is—carpeting. This fact may come as unwelcome news when one is poised with a sanding machine ready to "restore" the floor to its ancient glory, but the fact remains that in many nineteenth-century houses the floors were never meant to be seen and, consequently, were made of comparatively low-grade or nondecorative woods. If some visible wood on the floors is desired, however, there is absolutely no nonpedantic reason for not having it—even if it may not be strictly historically correct. The range of possible finishes is wide, from the sandpapering and clear-finishing of the original wood floor, whatever it may be, to overlaying it with more expensive wood finishes such as parquet blocks—which, incidentally, *were* used in the nineteenth century. Parquet flooring is now obtainable in the form of thin "tiles" about three-eighths of an inch thick but must be laid on a smooth surface; it will most likely be necessary, therefore, to have an intermediate layer of a half inch of plywood between them and the existing floor, unless the latter is completely smooth.

If the existing floor is to be exposed and the quality of the wood is not of the best, it must first be checked to see that it is reasonably smooth and does not tend to form dangerous splinters—for if it does it may be better covered up again. Unless the wood is to be painted (which is not generally to be recommended), its natural color will tend to determine the finished color of the floor—although here the careful use of stains and diluted stains can do much to adjust this if the real color is not very attractive in itself. Many commercial stains are over-colorful in themselves and tend to produce a caricature of the woods they are supposed to resemble, particularly when applied to wood that already has some color in it (i.e., "mahogany," which is too red, "oak," which is too yellow), but they can be modified by diluting them with turpentine and mixing in, perhaps, just a tiny drop of black paint. If this is done, however, a very accurate record of the proportions must be kept or an extra-large quantity should be mixed, so there will be no change of color if the batch runs out halfway across a floor. It is very easy to underestimate the amount of stain wash needed to cover a floor, especially when the wood is newly sanded and porous. Diluted stains are also useful for subtly tinting light or dark patches on floors until they match the surrounding areas.

For finishing natural, stained, or lightly stained wood floors there is generally nothing better than a matte or low-gloss clear sealant, from the point of view of both maintenance and appearance. Shellac and varnish are less successful, being too glossy and—in the case of shellac—easily marked by water. Here, as in many other places, glossy finishes should be avoided, since they tend to show up all the minute imperfections of a surface, plus all the dust particles that settle on it when it is drying.

EXPOSED BRICK WALLS. One of the great dramatic effects possible when rehabilitating an interior is, of course, the exposing of brickwork previously hidden behind plaster. Although this can easily be overdone, becoming a tiresome cliché, it can also be very attractive when used appropriately. As when "restoring" floors, however, one should carefully examine the quality of the surface to see whether, in fact, the bricks are exposable and, if not, the urge to be "original" should be firmly controlled. While opinions will differ as to how much "nature," in the form of roughnesses and irregularities, is permissible in a given context, if the color of the brickwork to be exposed is bad, or even questionable, it will certainly ruin the whole effect of the wall. In such cases, however, if the brickwork is otherwise acceptable, it may still be possible to get some of the effect originally intended by painting it—say white or off-white.

If clear sealants are being used on an exposed unpainted

indoor brick wall, any suspicion of gloss should again be avoided—otherwise the genuine material may begin to look like a plastic imitation. A very light sheen may, of course, help to take away from the appearance of extremely dry "corkiness," which, as already noted, results when the brickwork is cleaned by the sandblasting process, but it should not be overdone.

PLASTER WALLS AND CEILINGS. Many of the repairs to walls and ceilings can be done by the homeowner—provided, of course, that the existing plaster is in general firmly attached to the lathing—those thin wooden strips that support it from behind. Local cracks and holes can be filled with spackle that can be bought by the packet at the local hardware store and mixed in any quantity by adding water until it is about the same consistency as peanut butter. Apply it directly to the hole or crack with an artist's palette knife or spatula and push it in well before smoothing the surface. The surface should be allowed to bulge a little beyond the face of the surrounding plaster to allow for shrinkage when drying, and afterwards should be sandpapered lightly until it is completely flush. After painting, such a repair should be more or less invisible.

Repairs to cornices and other kinds of decoration are more complicated and, in addition to handiness, may require some ingenuity. The homeowner may be able to develop his own technique for casting plaster parts from spackle, but if not, the services will have to be sought of one of the few craftsmen who can still do this.

GENERAL DETAILS. There are many other items in a house that can be repaired or refinished by the handy amateur, and in many cases the only way to learn how to do it is to try. Many old houses, for instance, have fine paneling of hardwoods (i.e., mahogany, walnut, oak), which may have been damaged or covered with layers of paint or varnish, and it is often possible for the homeowner to bring them back to life by, first, finding out how to remove them—this will differ with each house and period—then repairing the cracks with glue while holding them together with clamps or tightened string, replacing them, and, finally, refinishing or repainting them. In addition to reading books on the subject, first-hand information can often be acquired by joining a local woodwork class or by talking with others who have faced the same problems. On the other hand, tasks such as the restoration of damaged gold-leaf decoration require a type of skill that can only result from long practice and are usually best left to the professional.

Each person must judge for himself just how far he can proceed in repairing, refinishing, or rehabilitating his house by his own efforts, for in the end this is really limited only by his ability to use his hands, his patience, and his inventiveness. Also, however—and this has been the main message of the book—he must make sure that the selected finishes are appropriate to the character of the house, just as he must judge for himself which of the features and details can or should be retained in the new interior. Here one cannot do better than end by quoting an outstanding designer of the nineteenth century, William Morris, whose advice still applies: "Have nothing in your house which you do not know to be useful or believe to be beautiful."

𒊹𒊹|*Glossary:*
Basic Architectural
and Building Terms

ARCHITRAVE

The lowest part of an entablature (see *Orders*) or, as more commonly used in connection with houses, the molded trim around a door or window opening.

BARGEBOARD

A projecting board, often decorated, that acts as trim to cover the ends of the structure where a pitched roof overhangs a gable.

bargeboard

BAY WINDOW

A projecting bay with windows that forms an extension to the floor space of the internal rooms. On the outside the bay should, properly, extend right down to ground level—as opposed to an Oriel window, which emerges from the building somewhere above ground level; the two terms, however, are frequently confused.

bay window

BEAM

A large horizontal structural member, usually of wood or metal, that spans between columns or supporting walls. It is

most often used to help carry the weight of a floor by supporting the joists, or to carry the weight of a wall above an opening.

BELT COURSE

A horizontal "belt" formed by a projecting course (or
courses) in a masonry wall for decorative purposes.

BLINDS

In old houses the term is used to denote an external or internal louvered wooden shutter that excludes direct sunlight
but admits light through a window. The external blind, by
intercepting the sun's heat *before* it passes through the glass of
the window, is still one of the best ways of keeping the interior
of a house cool. Internal blinds can also be quite effective and
attractive: in some houses they fold back into the wood paneling around the window to become almost invisible, and so any
mysterious knobs on the paneling should be investigated.

Now the term "blind" is generally applied to the roll-up or
Venetian variety and the wooden hinged types are incorrectly
referred to as "shutters" (which do not have louvers).

BOW WINDOW

A curved bay window taking the form of a segment of a
circle in plan.

BRACKET

A small projection, usually decorated, which supports or
appears to support a projecting cornice or lintel (see illustration
on page 81).

CAPITAL

The head of a column (see *Orders*).

CLAPBOARDS

Narrow, horizontal, overlapping wooden boards that form
the outer skin of the walls of many wood frame houses. The
horizontal lines of the overlaps, which generally are from four
to six inches apart in older houses—give the wall a distinctive

texture somewhat similar to that of a "lapstreak" or "clinker-built" boat.

CLASSICAL

A term used to describe the architecture of ancient Greece and Rome and also, more loosely, the later styles based on it (see also *Orders*). These later styles would include all the work of the Renaissance period in Europe and its later offshoots such as Georgian, Federal, Greek Revival, Renaissance Revival, Italianate, French Second Empire, and so forth.

The principal European nonclassical styles were Romanesque and Gothic, and these, together with certain medieval domestic details, inspired the Romanesque and Gothic Revival styles and the so-called Queen Anne style of the nineteenth century.

CLERESTORY WINDOWS

Windows located relatively high up in a wall that often tend to form a continuous band, as in the nave of a church. When used in a domestic context, the sills of such windows would be at least at eye level.

COLUMN

A vertical shaft or pillar that supports, or appears to support, a load (see *Orders*).

CONTEMPORARY

A word sometimes used to describe modern architecture (i.e., the Contemporary style). More properly it means simply "belonging to the same period" and has therefore been avoided, where possible, in this book in the interest of clarity.

CORBEL

A projection or building-out from a masonry wall, sometimes to support a load and sometimes for decorative effect.

CORINTHIAN

See *Orders*.

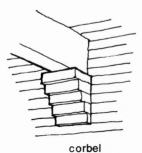

corbel

CORNER BOARD

One of the narrow vertical boards at the corner of a traditional wood frame building, into which the clapboards butt.

CORNICE

The top part of an entablature, usually molded and projecting (see *Orders*), or any continuous molded and projecting cap to a wall or window or door opening. Also, internally, a molded transition between wall and ceiling.

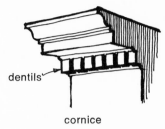

dentils

cornice

CURTAIN WALL

A light, non-load-bearing, weatherproof "skin" wall forming the outer face of a building and which usually takes the form of a metal grid with glass and opaque infill panels. It reached its height of popularity in the 1950's but since then, because of over-use or abuse, has declined sharply in favor. Although it has been handled on occasion with distinction, it has most often been used in the field of rehabilitation merely as a quick and cheap way to cover up an old building and transform it completely—but seldom into something better.

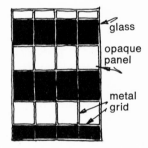

glass

opaque panel

metal grid

curtain wall

DADO

In houses, the lower part of an internal wall, when the wall has been divided horizontally by the use of different materials or treatments. If it consists of wood paneling it is sometimes referred to as the wainscot or wainscote.

dado

DENTIL

One of a series of small rectangular blocks, similar in effect to teeth, which are often found in the lower part of a cornice (see *Cornice* illustration).

DORIC

See *Orders.*

DORMER

A structure containing a vertical window (or windows) that projects through a pitched roof. The term can also be used to describe the window or windows.

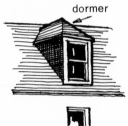

dormer

ELEVATION

A mechanically accurate, "head-on" drawing of a face of a building or object, without any allowance for the effect of the laws of perspective. Any measurement on an elevation will be in a fixed proportion, or scale, to the corresponding measurement on the real building.

The term is also used in land surveys for denoting the altitude of a point in relationship to a known height (i.e., sea level or a local bench mark).

elevation   perspective

ENGLISH BOND

See Chapter V, page 61.

ENTABLATURE

See *Orders.*

FASCIA

A flat board with a vertical face that forms the trim along the edge of a flat roof, or along the horizontal, or "eaves," sides of a pitched roof. The rain gutter is often mounted on it.

FLEMISH BOND

See Chapter V, page 61.

GABLE

The portion, above eaves level, of an end wall of a building with a pitched or gambrel roof. In the case of a pitched roof this takes the form of a triangle. The term is also used sometimes to refer to the whole end wall.

GAMBREL ROOF

See *Roof Types*.

HALF-BATH

Real estate shorthand for a small "bathroom" without— ironically—a bathtub, but sometimes with a shower. It is generally located on the ground floor of a house, or on a floor other than that of the main bathroom.

HIP ROOF

Also Hipped Roof (see *Roof Types*).

IONIC

See *Orders*.

JAMB

The vertical sides of an opening —usually for a door or window.

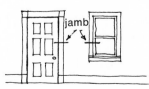

JOIST

One of the small horizontal wood beams that support the floors or ceilings of a house. They are set parallel to one another—usually from 1'-0" to 2'-0" apart—and span between supporting walls or larger wood beams.

LEADER

See *Rain Leader*.

LINTEL

A horizontal beam over an opening in a masonry wall, which carries the weight of the structure above.

MANSARD ROOF

See *Roof Types*.

MASONRY

Exterior wall material, such as brick or stone, which is laid up in small units.

MASSING

See Chapter II, page 18.

MOLDING

A decorative band or strip of material with a constant profile or section designed to cast interesting shadows. It is generally used in cornices and as trim around window and door openings.

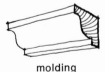

molding

MUNTIN

See *Window Parts*.

ORDERS

In classical architecture an Order consists of a *Column*, or shaft (with or without a base), its *Capital*, or head, and the horizontal *Entablature* above, which it supports (see illustration below). These were proportioned and decorated according to certain Modes, the three basic ones being established by the ancient Greeks—the Doric, the Ionic, and the Corinthian. These modes were later modified by the Romans, who added three more of their own—the Tuscan, the Roman Doric, and the Composite, the latter being a synthesis of the Greek Ionic and Corinthian orders. In practice these orders are most easily identified by their capitals, each of which has a distinctive form —particularly the Greek ones.

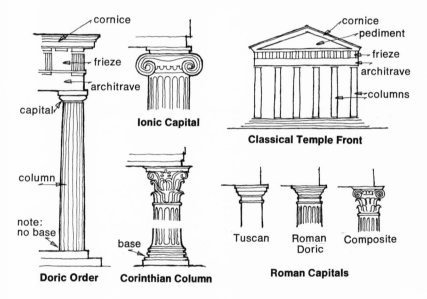

Apart from those of the Greek Revival style—which was a very conscious effort to reproduce the orders and details associated with the newly rediscovered architecture of ancient Greece —most of the "classical" details found in nineteenth-century houses tend to be borrowed from the Renaissance styles, which, in turn, were based on the architecture of ancient Rome. One is most likely to see in these houses, therefore, columns that are close or vague relatives of the Roman orders, and details such as arches that were a distinctively Roman contribution to classical architecture.

ORIEL WINDOW

A projecting bay with windows, which emerges from the building at a point above ground level. It is often confused with a bay window (see *Bay Window*).

oriel window

PANE

See *Window Parts*.

PARTITION

An internal wall usually of wood frame construction. It may be load-bearing or non-load-bearing.

PEDIMENT

A low triangular gable in classical architecture, formed by raising the top portion of the cornice of the entablature to follow the slope of the roof. (See *Orders* illustration.)

PERSPECTIVE DRAWING

A drawing of a building or an interior as the camera might see it, i.e. with the receding planes "vanishing" according to the laws of perspective. It is usually referred to simply as a "perspective" and, other than building a model, is one of the most realistic ways of illustrating a proposed design. (See also *Elevation* illustration.)

PILASTER

A flat-faced or half-round column which appears as if embedded in the surrounding wall and which projects slightly from it.

PITCH

The angle of slope of a roof, i.e., a 30° pitched roof, a low-pitched roof, a high-pitched roof, and so forth.

PLAN

A drawing representing a downward view of an object or, more commonly, a horizontal section of it. In the case of a floor of a house, it will show the disposition of the walls, partitions, rooms, doors, windows. (See also Chapter VII.)

PLANE

See Chapter II, pages 17–18.

POINTING

The outer, and visible, finish of the mortar between the bricks or stones of a masonry wall.

PROPORTION

See Chapter II, page 22.

RAFTER

One of the sloping joists in a pitched roof.

RAIN LEADER

A vertical pipe for conducting rainwater from the roof or gutter to the drain.

RISER

The vertical surface in a staircase between the treads.

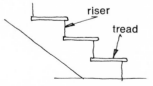

ROOF TYPES

Basically, roofs are either flat or pitched. The Monopitch, or Shed, roof is a type of pitched roof but with one slope only. The simplest

flat   shed

regular form of pitched roof has vertical
end walls that form gables; and if
the pitch is continued around the end
walls it is known as a Hipped roof. The
Gambrel and Mansard roofs have two
pitches and were developed in order
to have more headroom inside the
roof space: the Gambrel has vertical
gables on the end walls, but the Mansard
has the same roof profile on all four
sides, making it in effect a "Hipped
Gambrel."

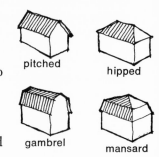

pitched

hipped

gambrel

mansard

SASH

See *Window Parts*.

SCALE

A full explanation of this term as applied to buildings and
spaces is given in Chapter II, pages 24–5. When applied to
a drawing or a model of a building it has a different, technical,
meaning denoting the size of the drawing or model in relation
to full-size building: i.e., scale: $\frac{1}{4}'' = 1'\text{-}0''$ means that one
quarter of an inch on the drawing represents one foot of the
actual building.

SECTION

A drawing representing a building, or part of a building,
as it would appear if cut through on a certain plane; in architectural drawings this plane is usually vertical, the horizontal
sections being referred to as plans. (See also Chapter VII, page
113.)

SHUTTERS

Small wooden "doors" on the outside of windows, originally
used for security purposes and now retained or installed mainly
for decorative effect. They are generally confused with external
blinds, which are somewhat similar in appearance but are lou-

vered, being intended for a different purpose—that of preventing direct sunlight, but allowing light, to enter the house. (See also *Blinds*).

SIDING

The narrow horizontal or vertical wood boards that form the outer face of the walls in a traditional wood frame house. Horizontal wood siding is also referred to as clapboards. The term "siding" is also more loosely used to describe any material that can be applied to the outside of a building as a finish.

SILL

The lowest horizontal member in a frame or opening for a window or door. Also, the lowest horizontal member in a framed wall or partition (see wall sill in illustration on page 32).

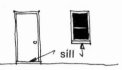

SOLDIER COURSE

A horizontal row of upright bricks used for variety and decorative effect in brickwork—often over window and door openings.

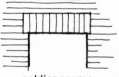

soldier course

SPACE

See Chapter II, pages 18–19.

SPANDREL

The space between an arch and a rectangle that encloses it.

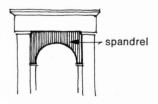

spandrel

STRUCTURAL WALL

Any wall that helps to support part of the load from floors, roofs, and so forth. Structural walls either go down to footings, or foundations in the ground, or rest on a substantial beam.

STUD

One of the upright members that extend from floor to ceiling in a wood frame wall or partition.

SURROUND

The molded trim around a door or window opening (see also *Architrave*).

TONE

See Chapter II, page 20.

TREAD

The horizontal surface of a step (see *Riser*).

WAINSCOT

Wood boarding or paneling on the lower part of an internal wall or partition (see also *Dado*).

WET WALL

A wall on one side of a bathroom or kitchen containing within it all the necessary plumbing and services.

WINDER

A tapered tread in a staircase. By using winders in place of a flat landing, the stair is enabled to climb as it turns, thereby saving space. Winders present a certain hazard, however, and most local building codes do not permit their use in new public stairs.

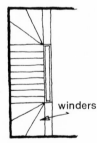

winders

WINDOW PARTS

The moving units of a window are known as Sashes and move within the fixed Frame. The Sash may consist of one large Pane of glass or may be subdivided into smaller Panes by thin members called Muntins or Glazing Bars. Sometimes in nineteenth-century

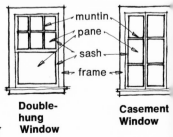

muntin
pane
sash
frame

Double-hung Window

Casement Window

houses windows are arranged side by side and divided by heavy vertical wood members called Mullions.

mullion

WORK TRIANGLE

An imaginary triangle drawn between the stove, sink, and refrigerator in a kitchen. It represents the paths most often taken when working in the kitchen, and the sum of its sides is a measure of the efficiency of the circulation—the smaller the better.

🌀🌀🌀| *Appendix A: Design Criteria for New Buildings in Historic Savannah*

APPLICATION OF CRITERIA

Within the historic area there is a predominance of similar design characteristics in particular blocks and/or squares. For example, a majority of buildings may have Savannah grey brick, have similar windows and porches, and be three stories in height. Even though there may be a variety of characteristics, each localized area tends to have a preponderance of special characteristics as well.

In order to preserve the integrity of the Old Savannah Area and the more localized characteristics found in various parts of the area, a number of design criteria have been developed by which individual structures may be compared and evaluated. The intent in developing these 16 criteria has been to identify specific design elements which, if repeated or echoed a sufficient number of times, will assure the maintenance and preservation of the architectural and historic character of the area. While providing guidelines for the restoration of existing structures, use of these criteria will also assure that new construction will blend reasonably well with the present character of the area.

Reprinted from *Historic Preservation Plan for the Central Area General Neighborhood Renewal Area, Savannah, Georgia* with the permission of the Housing Authority of Savannah and the cooperation of Eric Hill Associates, Planning Consultants.

The design criteria identify 16 characteristics of relatedness; each characteristic has been assigned a one-point value. In order for a proposed structure or a remodeling of an existing structure to be acceptable, it would have to achieve an evaluation rating of at least six points, indicating that at least six characteristics would be similar to those of a majority of the structures in the immediately surrounding area.

With the identification of these criteria, hopefully they will become working tools for the developer, architect, and client. Ideally, they should be studied and evaluated before design work begins so that the desired relationships can be established as design objectives, properly relating the individual building to the total environment.

In order for this process to function smoothly, clearly it will be necessary for the City of Savannah to establish a civic design commission or a historic area review board.

CRITERIA

1. *Height*—This is a mandatory criteria that new buildings be constructed to a height within ten percent of the average height of existing adjacent buildings.

RATIO PROPORTION   1 - 1 1/2

2. *Proportion of buildings' front facades*—The relationship between the width and height of the front elevation of the building.

WINDOW PROPORTION 2-1

3. *Proportion of openings within the facade*—The relationship of width to height of windows and doors.

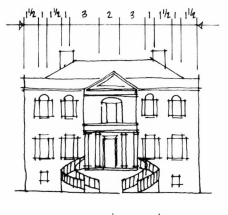

RHYTHM $1\frac{1}{2} \cdot 1 \cdot 1\frac{1}{2} \cdot 1 \cdot 3$

4. Rhythm of solids to voids in front facade—Rhythm being an ordered recurrent alternation of strong and weak elements. Moving by an individual building, one experiences a rhythm of masses to openings.

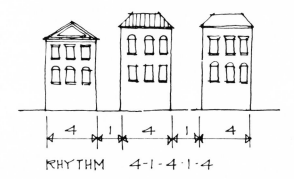

RHYTHM $4 \cdot 1 \cdot 4 \cdot 1 \cdot 4$

5. Rhythm of spacing of buildings on streets—Moving past a sequence of buildings, one experiences a rhythm of recurrent building masses to spaces between them.

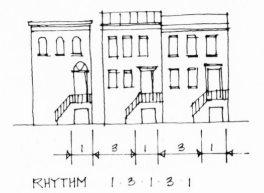

RHYTHM   1 · 3 · 1 · 3 · 1

6. *Rhythm of entrance and/or porch projections*—The relationships of entrances to sidewalks. Moving past a sequence of structures, one experiences a rhythm of entrances or porch projections at an intimate scale.

MATERIAL / BRICK
TEXTURE / RAKED JOINT
COLOR / RED BK., GRAY TRIM

7. *Relationship of materials*—Within an area, the predominant material may be brick, stone, stucco, wood siding, or other material.

8. *Relationship of textures*—The predominant texture may be smooth (stucco) or rough (brick with tooled joints) or horizontal wood siding, or other textures.

9. *Relationship of color*—The predominant color may be that of a natural material or a painted one, or a patina colored by time. Accent or blending colors of trim is also a factor.

10. *Relationship of architectural details*—Details may include cornices, lintel, arches, quoins, balustrades, wrought iron work, chimneys, etc.

11. *Relationship of roof shapes*—The majority of buildings may have gable, mansard, hip, flat roofs, or others.

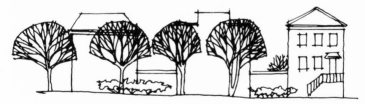

WALLS & LANDSCAPING   CONTINUOUS

12. *Walls of continuity*—Physical ingredients such as brick walls, wrought iron fences, evergreen landscape masses, building facades, or combinations of these, form continuous, cohesive walls of enclosure along the street.

13. *Relationship of landscaping*—There may be a predominance of a particular quality and quantity of landscaping. The concern here is more with mass and continuity.

GROUND COVERING

14. *Ground cover*—There may be a predominance in the use of brick pavers, cobble stones, granite blocks, tabby, or other materials.

UNITS OF SCALE

15. *Scale*—Scale is created by the size of construction and architectural detail which relate to the size of man. Scale is also determined by building mass and how it relates to open space. The predominant element of scale may be brick or stone units, windows or door openings, porches and balconies, etc.

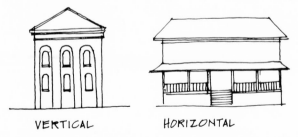

VERTICAL   HORIZONTAL

16. *Directional expression of front elevation*—Structural shape, placement of openings, and architectural details may give a predominantly vertical, horizontal, or a non-directional character to the building's front facade.

214

Criteria

Height
Proportion of buildings' front facades
Proportion of openings within the facade
Rhythm of solids to voids in front facade
Rhythm of spacing of buildings on streets
Rhythm of entrance and/or porch projections
Relationship of materials
Relationship of textures
Relationship of color
Relationship of architectural details
Relationship of roof shapes
Walls of continuity
Relationship of landscaping
Ground cover
Scale
Directional expression of front elevation

The newer house in the center does not relate to its neighbors in height, proportion, color, materials, details, rhythms, or landscaping. According to criteria, it receives only one point for relation of setback.

Although a handsome building, this new structure does not relate well with older existing structures. In another location it might be entirely acceptable. According to criteria it relates in setback (6) only.

Although these three detached houses have distinctly different styles, there is a sense of relatedness.

1. Proportion of building facades
2. Heights
3. Walls of enclosure

4. Rhythms of entrances
5. Landscaping
6. Details
7. Proportion of openings

216

In a tightly spaced block, there is variation of housing
facades, yet houses are well related.

1. Height   4. Rhythms of entrances
2. Proportion of facades   5. Rhythms of spacing
3. Proportion of openings   6. Landscaping

A large institutional building next to a residential row relates well because its massing has been broken down into
three increments which are sympathetic in scale to the
residential row. It relates in height, setback, landscaping,
proportion of openings, wall of continuity, and color.

*Rather dissimilarly styled houses relate well while form-
ing a wall of enclosure of space to enclose a corner of
a square. Relatedness is expressed in:*

1. *Details—porches*   5. *Colors*
2. *Height*   6. *Positions of openings*
3. *Proportion of facades* 7. *Walls of enclosure*
4. *Landscaping*

This demonstrates good relationship between a church complex and a residence, showing:

1. Materials
2. Colors
3. Textures
4. Details—arches
5. Landscaping—earth cover
6. Closure of space

Two houses have different exterior materials yet relate well because of:

1. Height
2. Rhythms of spacing
3. Rhythms of entrances
4. Proportion of buildings
5. Proportions of openings
6. Landscaping

꩹꩹꩹|*Appendix B: Building Planning Section of HUD'S Manual PG-50*

(Minimum Floor Areas and Other Requirements)

PURPOSE AND INTENT

These physical guidelines for the rehabilitation of existing residential properties have been developed to provide minimum design and construction criteria on a national basis. The provisions are intended to serve as an important aid in carrying out the objectives of Federal and local programs for neglected and run-down properties. These objectives seek the large-scale physical, social, and economic regeneration of neighborhoods that have, in general, deteriorated seriously.

THE FORMAT

Outline designations prefixed by the letter R, that is, R400, are minimum performance provisions. These provisions use the word "shall" to mean that local rehabilitation standards must meet at least this level of performance. Good practice items that provide useful specific information are designated by the letter G, that is, G401, and use the word "should." These items merit serious consideration in establishing local standards for projects, urban renewal, or code enforcement areas, but are on an optional basis.

R400

OBJECTIVE: To assure a living unit which provides for a healthful environment and complete living facilities arranged and equipped for suitable and desirable living conditions commensurate with the type and quality of the property under consideration.

R401

SPACE STANDARDS

R401-1
General

R401-1.1

Provide each living unit with space necessary for suitable living, sleeping, cooking and dining accommodations, storage, laundry and sanitary facilities; also, provide space of such size and dimensions so as to permit placement of furniture and essential equipment.

R401-1.2

Habitable rooms in basements or below grade intended for year-round occupancy shall comply with building planning standards in the same manner as rooms above grade. See R402.

R401-2

Room Sizes: The size of rooms shown in Table R4-1 shall be minimum for the subdividing of existing spaces or for the construction of new rooms. Unremodeled existing rooms where considered of adequate size and arrangement for the intended function by the proper authority are acceptable.

GUIDES

G401-1

For existing work dimensions for interior spaces are based upon measurements taken between finished floor, wall, ceiling or partition surfaces.

The area occupied by a stair or by closets should not be included in the determination of required room area.

Table R4-1

ROOM SIZES

Name of Space(1)	Minimum Area (Sq. Ft.) (2)			Least Dimension(2)
	O-BR LU	1 & 2 BR LU	3 or more BR LU	
LR	NA	140	150	10'-0"
DR	NA	80	100	7'-8"
K	NA	50	60	5'-4"
K'ette	20	25	40	3'-6"
BR (Double)	NA	110	110	8'-8"
BR (Single)	NA	70	70	7'-0"
LR-DA	NA	180	200	(3)
LR-DA-K	NA	220	250	(3)
LR-DA-SL	220	NA	NA	(3)
LR-SL	190	NA	NA	(3)
K-DA	80	80	110	(3)
K'ette-DA	60	60	90	(3)

NOTES:

(1) Abbreviations:

LU = Living Unit   K'ette = Kitchenette
LR = Living Room   BR = Bedroom
DR = Dining Room   SL = Sleeping Area
DA = Dining Area   NA = Not Applicable
K = Kitchen   O-BR = No separate bedroom

(2) Variations to these areas and dimensions may be permitted when existing partitions preclude precise compliance, and the available area or dimensions do not hinder furniture placement and the normal use of the space.

(3) The least dimension of each room function applies, except for the overlap or double use of space in combination rooms.

G401-2

The floor areas given in Table R4-1 are minimum for healthy occupancy in order to reflect maximum construction economy but the combining of these minimums in planning living units is not recommended. Only plan layouts which provide successfully for closet and window location, door swings and furniture placement will determine whether minimum space will result in acceptable livability.

R401-3

Ceiling Heights: Ceiling heights shall permit the average person to move about comfortably, and create no unpleasant sensation because of the ceiling being of insufficient height.

R401-4

Privacy and Arrangement

R401-4.1

A degree of privacy shall be provided commensurate with suitable living conditions by means of the proper location of exterior openings to exterior conditions, and by the interior arrangement of rooms.

R401-4.2

Access to all parts of a living unit shall be possible without passing through a public hall.

R401-4.3

Every water closet, bathtub or shower of a living unit shall be installed in a bathroom or toilet compartment which will afford privacy to the occupant.

R401-4.4

A bathroom shall not be used as a passageway to a habitable room, hall, basement or to the exterior.

GUIDES

G401-3

The ceiling heights for habitable rooms, bathrooms and public and private halls should be at least the following:

Habitable Rooms—7 ft.-6 in.

Bathrooms, toilet compartments, utility rooms—6 ft.-8 in.

Public Corridors—7 ft.-8 in.

Halls within living units—7 ft. clear

Suspended Ceilings or panels—7 ft.-4 in.

Sloping ceiling—no portion less than 7 ft.-0 in.

G401-4

Where the access to an existing bathroom is through a bedroom in living units having more than one bedroom, this planning arrangement should be accepted if it is judged to be acceptable to the market.

A bathroom should not be separated from all bedrooms of a living unit by locating it a full story above or below the bedrooms.

A bedroom should not be used as the only means of access to another bedroom or habitable room.

R401-5

Kitchen Facilities: Each living unit shall have a specific kitchen space, which contains a sink with counter work space and has hot and cold running water, adequate space for installing cooking and refrigeration equipment, and for storing cooking utensils.

R401-6

Bath Facilities: Complete bathing and sanitary facilities shall be provided within each living unit; they shall consist of a water-closet, a tub or shower, and a lavatory. Provide an adequate supply of hot water to the tub or shower stall and lavatory, and cold water to all fixtures. Arrangement of fixtures shall provide for the comfortable use of each fixture and permit at least a 90° door swing. Wall space shall be available for a mirror or medicine cabinet and for towel bars.

R401-7

Space for Laundry Facilities: Adequate space shall be provided for laundry equipment within each living unit, off of a public corridor, or in a basement or other suitable public space for the use of all occupants of a building. Where nearby public commercial laundries are available, consideration may be given as to the extent residents of the project can be expected to use them in determining laundry space needs.

GUIDES

G401-5
Minimum areas of kitchen storage space should be as follows:
  a. Total shelving in wall and base cabinets—30 sq. ft.
  b. Drawer area—5 sq. ft.
  c. Usable storage shelving in cooking range or under sink may be counted in the total shelving needed.
  Kitchen storage space of living units having two or more bedrooms should be appropriately increased in total area to accommodate the needs of more occupants.

R401-8
Closets and General Storage: Clothes closet space shall be provided within bedrooms or conveniently located nearby. In addition, each living unit shall have a suitable space within the unit or a locked space elsewhere within the building for general storage.

GUIDES

G401-8
Clothes closet space should be provided at a minimum of 4 sq. ft. per adult or youth. For hanging clothes efficiently a shelf and hanging rod should be provided, preferably in closets of not less than 2 ft. deep.
  It is recommended that clothes closet space not be located within a kitchen.
  The minimum volume of general storage space for each living unit should be 100 cu. ft. and should be appropriately increased for 3 or 4 bedroom living units.

R402
LIGHT AND VENTILATION

R402-1
General: Provide a healthful environment and an acceptable degree of comfort within all rooms and hallways of the dwelling by having sufficient light and ventilation, and provide natural ventilation for structural spaces to minimize conditions conducive to decay and deterioration.

R402-2
Habitable Rooms

R402-2.1
All habitable rooms, except kitchens, shall have natural light, provided by means of windows, glazed doors, or skylights. A glass area of at least 10 percent of the floor area shall be provided for new or remodeled rooms, or other spaces.[1]

R402-2.2
An acceptable means of natural ventilation shall exist or be provided for all habitable spaces, except that for kitchens a mechanical ventilation system may be substituted. A ventilation area of 5 percent of the floor area of the space shall be provided.

R402-2.3
Artificial light shall be provided and so distributed as to assure healthful conditions and satisfactory illumination in all rooms.

R402-2.4
Kitchens shall have artificial light provided. Ventilation shall be provided by either mechanical ventilation, or if by natural means—5 percent of floor area but not less than 3 sq. ft. area.

GUIDES

G402-2
Where an interior room without its own source of natural light and ventilation is adjacent to an outside room having both, con-

---

[1] An existing habitable room not disturbed in the rehabilitation which is deficient or without natural light can be considered acceptable provided this is judged by proper authority to have market acceptance.

sideration should be given to its acceptance as a habitable room, calculated on the basis of the combined floor area of the two rooms, where the separating wall between them has an opening either 6 ft. wide or is 70 percent as wide as the inside room.

R402-3
Bathrooms and Toilet Compartments: Artificial light shall be provided. Provide ventilation by mechanical means or if by natural means—5 percent of floor area but not less than 1½ sq. ft. area.

R402-4
Public Spaces: Artificial light shall be provided in all public spaces.

R402-4.1
Public Entrance Spaces: Provide either natural ventilation of at least 5 percent of floor area or mechanical ventilation.

R402-5
Ventilation of Utility Spaces: Utility spaces which contain heat producing, air conditioning and other equipment shall be ventilated to the outer air, and air from such spaces shall not be recirculated to other parts of the building.

R402-6
Ventilation of Structural Spaces: Natural ventilation of spaces such as attics and enclosed basementless spaces shall be provided by openings of sufficient size to overcome dampness and minimize the effect of conditions conducive to decay and deterioration of the structure, and to prevent excessive heat in attics. Exterior ventilation openings shall be effectively screened where needed.

R403
Doors and Access Openings: Provide openings adequate in size to admit furniture and equipment to all spaces and to permit inspection for repair and maintenance.

G402-3
Ventilation of bathrooms in small buildings is sometimes accomplished by a gravity-type vent equipped with a wind-driven roof ventilator above the roof level.

G402-4
Public hallways and unenclosed stairways should be provided with either natural ventilation (at least 5 percent of floor area) or mechanical ventilation. Enclosed public corridors should be ventilated mechanically.

R403-1
Exterior Doors: Exterior doors shall have safe locks.

R403-2
Interior Doors: Provide a door for each opening to a bedroom, bathroom or toilet compartment; with a locking device on bath and toilet compartment doors.

G403-1
Exterior doors should be at least the following sizes:

	Width	*Height*	
a. Main entrance door	3'-0"(1)	6'-6"	
b. Service doors	2'-6"	6'-6"	
c. Garage doors, 1 car	8'-0"	6'-4" clear opening	
d. Garage doors, 2 car	12'-0"	6'-4" clear opening	

(1) Where serving 12 or more Living Units = 3'-4"

G403-2
Interior doors should be at least the following size:
  a. Habitable rooms, 2 ft.-6 in. wide.
  b. Bathrooms, toilet compartments and closets other than linen and broom, 2 ft.-0 in. wide.
  c. Service stair doors, 2 ft.-6 in. wide.
  d. Cased openings, 2 ft.-6 in. wide.

e. To public stairway enclosures, single door = 3 ft.-0 in. wide; double = 2 ft.-4 in. wide.

f. Height of all interior doors, 6 ft.-6 in.

Attic and Basementless Spaces. Access to attics should be provided by means of conveniently located scuttles or a disappearing or permanently installed stairway. For attic and basementless spaces, the minimum access opening should be 14 × 22 inches. However, if either are to contain mechanical equipment, the access opening shall be of sufficient size to permit the removal and replacement of the equipment.

R404
STAIRWAYS

R404-1
General: All stairways shall provide safety of ascent and descent, and stairs and landings shall be arranged to permit adequate headroom and space for the passage of furniture and equipment.

R404-2
Existing Stairways[1]: Existing stairways in sound condition to remain or to be repaired shall not be to any serious extent below minimum standards of good practice as to rise and run of steps, headroom, obstructions, stair width, landings, or railing protection.

R404-3
New Stairways[1]: New stairways to be constructed shall comply with standards of good practice and be appropriate to the building and occupant load.

R405
CORRIDORS AND HALLWAYS

R405-1
General: Corridors and hallways shall provide adequate, safe and unobstructed circulation from living units or other spaces to various means of exit.

[1] See R502 for related conditions.

G404

Minimum standards for good practice in the planning and construction of stairways are contained in Chapter 4 of the MPS for Multifamily Housing (FHA No. 2600).

R406

ELEVATORS: Where provided, an elevator shall furnish convenient and safe ascent and descent to all living units and service areas. The character and type of elevator service and equipment should be appropriate to the building being rehabilitated and to its occupants.

R407

EXTERIOR APPURTENANCES

R407-1

All exterior appurtenances or accessory structures which serve no useful purpose, or those in a deteriorated condition which are not economically repairable, shall be removed. Such structures include porches, terraces, entrance platforms, garages, carports, walls, fences, miscellaneous sheds.

G405
Corridors and Hallways

G405-1

Corridors Having Access to Exit in Two Directions. The distance of travel from the entrance door of any living unit to an enclosed stairway, horizontal exit or exterior door should not exceed 100 feet.

Where a stairway is not separately enclosed and is open to a corridor or mezzanine, the distance of travel should include the travel on the stairway and the travel from the stairway to reach an outside door in addition to the distance to reach the stairway.

G405-2

Corridors or Hallways Having Access to Exit in One Direction. The distance of travel from the entrance door of any living unit to an exit in one direction should not exceed 30 feet, or if to an unenclosed stairway should not exceed 20 feet.

G405-3

Hallways providing access to stairways and serving more than one and less than six living units should be not less than 3 ft.-6 in. wide. Corridors serving more than six living units should be at least 5 ft. wide, with additional width at elevators being desirable.

G406

Elevator Service: Four story buildings should have one or more elevators where there are six or more living units per floor and where the continued acceptance of the property would be doubtful if there were no elevator service.

R408
TRASH AND GARBAGE DISPOSAL

R408-1

Every dwelling and multifamily building shall be supplied with a means of disposal or removal of trash and garbage.

R408-2

Where disposal will not take place promptly there shall be a convenient and appropriate temporary and sanitary storage for trash and garbage provided, which is inaccessible to rodents.

R409
NOISE CONTROL: (See G409 below)

GUIDES

G406

Buildings of more than four stories having six or more living units per floor should have appropriate elevator service provided.

G408

Where a flue-fed incinerator is used for disposal of waste materials, hoppers should not open directly into a public corridor, but open in a closet or room of not less than 20 sq. ft. in area, which has a self-closing door.

G409

Noise Control

G409-1

Where there is revised planning and *new* construction contemplated of floors and partitions between living units and between living units and public and service spaces, consideration should be given to using noise reduction and noise isolation techniques in order to provide acoustic separation and auditory privacy. The minimum sound transmission class (STC) rating of the construction for such purposes should be 45 for airborne noise.[1] For structure-borne or impact noise, the impact noise ratio (INR) should be in a range from +5 to −5.[2]

G409-2

Design and Construction Suggestions. Where practical, functional areas of high noise should be separated from areas of quiet. Clothes or storage closets are useful separators.

Extend partitions to solid floor-ceiling construction and not terminate at hung ceilings.

Caulk and wrap pipe and seal around ductwork where they penetrate sound-impeding partitions and floors. Line ducts near registers or grilles, and at fan discharge.

Balance and mount motors, fans and other equipment.

Where kitchens or bathrooms are located back-to-back give special attention to the construction to reduce noise from plumbing fixtures, and through medicine cabinets.

Where living units are adjacent to high noise areas such as boiler rooms or other mechanical equipment, the construction separating the spaces should provide a greater noise resistance than normal room separations.

---

[1] STC as determined by ASTM E90–66T.
[2] INR as classified by FHA No. 750; "Impact Noise Control in Multifamily Buildings," 1963.

༺ཉ༻ Index

i

A NOTE ABOUT THE AUTHOR

George Stephen was born in Aberdeen, Scotland, in 1926. He studied at the Aberdeen College of Architecture and the Architectural Association School of Architecture in London, and served for three and a half years in the Royal Engineers and Royal Army Education Corps. Before coming to the United States he practiced architecture in Edinburgh from 1957 to 1963. From 1963 to 1965 he practiced in Boston. In 1965 he joined the staff of the Boston Redevelopment Authority as South End Project Designer. Since that same year he has been Director of Rehabilitation Design for the Authority. He received citations in a competition for municipal offices in Northern Ireland (1956) and in the Annual Design Awards (urban design) of the American Registered Architects (1970) for work done for the Boston Redevelopment Authority.

A NOTE ON THE TYPE

The text of this book is set in Electra, a typeface designed by W. A. Dwiggins for the Mergenthaler Linotype Company and first made available in 1935. Electra cannot be classified as either "modern" or "old style." It is not based on any historical model, and hence does not echo any particular period or style of type design. It avoids the extreme contrast between "thick" and "thin" elements that marks most modern faces, and is without eccentricities which catch the eye and interfere with reading. In general, Electra is a simple, readable typeface which attempts to give a feeling of fluidity, power, and speed.

Composed, printed, and bound by The Colonial Press Inc., Clinton, Massachusetts.

Typography and binding design by Christine Aulicino.